Happy
Birthday

7/5/16
To my dear Vicki,
I thought this would
be interesting since you'd
like to live on a boat
some day. I personally
know the author.
Best wishes on
your dream.
Love, Mom

Life at the End of a Rope

of a Rope

All About Living On Boats

Anthony Alcock

LIFE AT THE END OF A ROPE

Published by Ocean Air Living.

www.oceanairliving.com

Author services by Pedernales Publishing, LLC.
www.pedernalespublishing.com

Cover design: Jose Ramirez and Barbara Rainess

Library of Congress Control Number: 2015921299

ISBN 978-0-9971622-0-2 Paperback Edition
ISBN 978-0-9971622-2-6 Hardcover Edition
ISBN 978-0-9971622-1-9 Digital Edition

Printed in the United States of America

"There's nothing—absolutely nothing—half so much worth doing as messing about in boats."

Kenneth Grahame, *The Wind In The Willows*

CONTENTS

Introduction 11

Chapter 1: Initial Exposure 13

   HIATUS II 13

      Introduction to Living Aboard 17

      Downsizing 21

      Finding my Sea Legs 21

      The Maiden Voyage 24

Chapter 2: Over three decades later 29

   HIATUS IV 29

      Second Time 34 years later 33

Chapter 3: Adventures on the High Seas 39

      Personal Experiences 41

      Best Boating Experience Ever 44

      A few "Misadventures" 46

      Stormy Return 48

      Lost in the Fog 49

      Dealing with Heavy Seas 51

      Grand Larceny on the High Seas 53

Chapter 4: All About Boats 55

Selecting the right kind of floating home 57

Barges (Canal boats) 58

Houseboats 59

Powerboats 59

Sailboats 60

Deciding where you should put it.................62

Chapter 5: Keeping Your Boat Afloat............................65

Things to Consider.................................67

Cost 67

Mooring/Slip fees 68

Utilities..68

Taxes...69

Insurance 69

Boating Rules and Regulations.................70

Safety..71

Maintenance.......................................72

Servicing..75

System Checks 76

Cleaning..76

Comfort 79

Chapter 6: Captains, World Cruisers, & Vagabonds....81

True stories of others who have chosen this
lifestyle...83

The Rigneys 85

The Andreottis 93

CONTENTS

The Eells.................................... 105

Rouillard & Huber................................. 113

Megan Rogers 119

The Cassons.................................... 125

Ben Green.................................... 135

The Brewers.................................... 141

The Howeys 151

A Summary of Living Aboard.................................... 161

Boat Terminology – Simplified.................................... 163

INTRODUCTION

*"The thing about boats is, you can always sell them
if you don't like them.*

"You can't sell your kids."

Lin Pardey

September of 2013 marked the beginning of my living aboard a yacht for the second time in my life. This short book is a partial autobiographical account of my own personal experiences while living on a boat and some general guidelines on choosing the right boat for you and where to put it. I also discuss what it takes to keep your boat afloat.

If you are new to the boating world and thinking of buying a boat, whether or not you intend to live on it, this little book will probably answer a lot of questions that you wouldn't even think to ask.

My prior, and first experience, in the late seventies, was a four-year midlife crisis hiatus following a financial and emotional meltdown with the divorce of my second wife, the mother of my children. Some 34 years later, I once again found myself back living aboard a yacht.

In this book I attempt to address the many pros and cons of living aboard, and the inevitable adventures and misadventures that come with it. These include the newfound freedom of living without most of our material stuff while learning to manage the endless challenges of a home that is essentially a floating bathtub.

I begin with a summary of my personal experiences, examine what kind of craft to buy and where to put it, some financial considerations, rules, safety, and the inevitable maintenance needed to stay afloat.

I have dedicated a chapter to various others who have chosen this lifestyle, be it out of financial necessity, the excitement and pleasure associated with simply living aboard a boat, or because they plan to realize their dream to cruise the world. Each of them have their own story to tell.

Lastly, I have included a brief appendix on some of the basic boat terminology.

I hope that you get as much pleasure from reading this little book as I did from writing it.

1 | INITIAL EXPOSURE

HIATUS II

HIATUS II

1961 Chris-Craft 36' Offshore Cruiser

A 36' wooden craft with "lapstrake" construction, she was originally built as a sport fishing boat. (Lapstrake means overlapping horizontal wooden stringers as seen in photo above.)

Main Salon

Original sport fishing boat before modifications

Work-in-Progress

The prior owner, Bill Sargent, did extensive modifications to extend both the cabin (main salon) and the flybridge to convert it to a very comfortable live-aboard. A wooden boat, using lapstrake construction, she was a very seaworthy vessel that handled up to 10' seas. The main salon was retrofitted with a small but efficient fireplace fed with charcoal brickets. There were three steps down to the dinette, galley, and small closets. A basic bathroom was across from the galley. Up front was the small but cozy V-Berth "stateroom."

INTRODUCTION TO LIVING ABOARD

By the mid-seventies, I had become accustomed to a life of relative luxury. As a successful businessman, I lived on a modest ranch in Malibu, California with my wife, two children, a live-in housekeeper, horses, and several dogs. We had good investments, including beachfront rental income property.

It is surprising how quickly an acrimonious relationship can cause everything to completely unravel, which it did. My ex-wife-to-be moved to San Diego, taking our children with her and, with the sale of our ranch, I explored my options.

I was looking to rent an apartment near my business office in Marina del Rey, California and was somewhat disenchanted with the options available. By chance one day, I drove by a yacht broker and looked at several boats that were for sale. Intrigued with the notion of buying one to live on, I began a whole new adventure.

Born and raised in a land-locked, industrial city in England, my only exposure to the ocean was on the annual family vacation to the "seaside." So, my only "boating" experience was aboard the Queen Elizabeth Liner, on which I migrated to the USA in 1965. Thus, to say I was naïve about boats is an understatement.

As boats depreciate in value very rapidly, the reasons for which I discovered later, I decided to look for an appropriate used vessel. However, I quickly determined that finding a slip in which to put the boat was, at that time, a far bigger challenge.

Marina del Rey, an affluent seaside community, is the world's largest man-made small craft harbor, situated about 20 miles from downtown Los Angeles. It consists of 19 marinas with capacity for 5,300 boats and is home port to approximately 6,500 boats. Each marina is separately managed under strict leases from the county.

The renowned island of Catalina, some 26 miles offshore from this harbor, is a favorite destination for many boaters.

In the mid-seventies, with the economy booming, all slips were occupied with long waiting lists for new tenants. Not all marinas permitted "live-aboard" tenants, and those that did had even longer waiting lists of up to five years. It appeared that exploring an option to buy and live on a boat was not meant to be! I had telephoned all but one marina operator and received the same message, "Sorry, we have no slips available."

With low expectations, I called the last name on my list, Fiji Marine, a boat dealership that also had some 200 slips which they rented. The sales manager at first gave me the same negative response, but then hesitated and informed me of a yacht for sale, which, if I purchased, would come with "live-aboard" privileges. I told him that I would be right there to see the vessel.

It was late-morning on a beautiful Spring California day as the sales manager and I walked down the boat ramp of E-dock in H-basin. The sun glinted off the white boat hulls, halyards of sailboats clinked in the gentle breeze, and seagulls soared above us.

As we strolled down the dock, we passed by several different craft and my anticipation and excitement heightened. I really knew nothing about boats, only that the powerboat I was to view was a 36-foot 1961 Chris-Craft offshore cruising powerboat (whatever that meant).

Suddenly we were there at Slip E19. Passing by the bow (the pointy front end), we walked toward the stern (rear end). Sitting on the back deck, sipping champagne with a beautiful young lady, Patty, later to become his wife, was the owner, Bill Sargent. I assume he knew we were coming because he reached out a hand and said "Welcome aboard."More champagne was poured and a quick tour began. The spacious rear deck led into the main salon (living room) complete with a mini-charcoal-fed fireplace. Two steps down were a small dinette and galley (kitchen) and forward was the main stateroom (bedroom). Above all of this, via a ladder, was a flybridge with seating, steering wheel, and a lot of confusing instruments for running the vessel.

The decision to buy this boat was made even before the tour ended. Within ten minutes of boarding, I said "I'll take it." Somewhat surprised, Bill, the seller, accepted my full-price offer and a new chapter in my life began. The boat's name, *HIATUS II*, seemed appropriate as it represented "Time Out" after my second marriage, so I kept the boat's name.

Upon reflection, I really had very little knowledge about boats. There are, of course, two main categories; power and sail. Typically, a powerboat will afford the owner about twice the "living space" over the same size sailing vessel, and that choice was already made for me. Boats are constructed out of wood, fiberglass, aluminum, or steel, but most small craft today have fiberglass hulls. My new home, built in 1961, was of wood lapstrake construction, where the hull is built from horizontal, overlapping wooden laths. As I found out later, this makes for a very stable ride in heavy seas. Originally, this craft had a very small cabin and was essentially designed for fishing with a large open rear deck. The owner, Bill, had given it many hours of TLC and had extended the cabin to provide a good size stateroom and a larger flybridge. There were many personal touches that reflected his love and appreciation for this classic Chris-Craft, including a small, working Scottish fireplace surrounded with decorative tile in the main stateroom.

DOWNSIZING

"At sea, I learned how little a person needs, not how much."
Robin Lee Graham

Transitioning from living in a house (in my case a ranch) to living on a boat required a major reduction in the amount of "stuff" that I kept. Essentially, if it won't fit in your car, then there is no room for it on your boat. All the creature comforts of home: toys, collectibles, furniture, china, crystal, etc., had to go. Of course this also meant my riding lawn mower and a large collection of power tools. A few selected items were loaned indefinitely to friends, but most of it was sold or given away. This turned out to be very therapeutic, as most of us collect stuff that we really don't need, or even want, any more. It was surprising to me how little one really needs to get by. "Simplify" became my new motto.

FINDING MY SEA LEGS

The first few weeks living aboard *HIATUS II* were a major adjustment after my life on a sprawling ranch in Malibu. The 1961 Chris-Craft quickly became my home and cozy nest. Being in close proximity (a few feet) from one's neighbors, especially if they also lived aboard, brought with it a whole new set of challenges.

Privacy, or the lack thereof, becomes a high priority. Most live-aboards have mutual respect for each other and, in general, don't have loud sound systems and keep their banter at a comfortably low level. Of course, there are always a few "trailer trash" types who seem to always test your patience.

Even while securely tied up in the dock, all boats make some noises. Dock lines moan as the wind or tide move the boat around, small waves make slapping sounds against the hull, and other creaking sounds emanate from various parts of the boat as the waters jostle it around. Wooden boats like this, my first one *HIATUS II*, are particular noisy. Most modern boats have fiberglass hulls that, for the most part, make little noise.

Many boat people who live aboard use the dock facilities for toilets and ablutions which requires trekking back and forth via the dock at all hours. This is a consideration if your boat slip is close to the ramp between the shore and the dock, as the foot traffic will be greater.

Over the course of the first week or so, I became aware of the unexpected activities of my neighbor, Jovan, a "part-time" live-aboard" whose boat occupied the slip directly across from mine (the bow of my boat faced his). It seemed that a never-ending stream of women were coming and going to his boat, many of them quite vocal about their feelings toward him; not always positive. Regardless, it appeared he was quite "the lady's man," and somehow the women were drawn to his boat like bees to honey. Clearly, in my newfound and somewhat lonely bachelorhood, I needed to meet this fellow and understand his charm. This I did and we became close friends.

The late seventies, was the age of women seeking freedom and equality, especially in their relationships with men. I quickly realized that the timing for my new bachelorhood was fortuitous. I will be forever indebted to my friend Jovan, who helped me adjust to my new life and reclaim a lot of my self-esteem. We enjoyed some absolutely wonderful and rewarding experiences that I will never forget. Far from seeking any meaningful relationships with women, I welcomed my newfound freedom. It gave me the opportunity to re-assess life's priorities, which I found emotionally very gratifying.

This was also the "Disco Era" and a local bar, Tiffany's, was in full swing with popular music by the BEE GEEs, ABBA, Donna Summer, Elton John, etc. They provided Disco Dance lessons and nightly dancing under one of those classic rotating mirrored ceiling balls. Also, nearby, was the Jockey Club, a private, pretentious pick-up joint on the top floor of a nearby building that was known as a "hot place" to meet. Within walking distance, centered in Marina del Rey's fishing village, was one of the earlier T.G.I. Fridays with its raised four-sided bar, perfectly designed for meeting new "friends."

THE MAIDEN VOYAGE

After settling in to my new home, it was time to do a real trip. I had taken her out a couple of times just outside the breakwater, and I felt somewhat comfortable piloting my home through the waves. A good friend of mine, my scuba diving partner, Myrna, equally as unskilled as myself around boats, agreed to accompany me on a trip to Catalina Island. From my boat slip in Marina del Rey, the island is about thirty miles away with a variety of moorings and anchorages available. On the southeast tip is the well-known town of Avalon. We decided to look for an anchorage or mooring somewhat closer.

If I had known then what I know today, we would never have left the dock. They say that "ignorance is bliss" and, in hindsight, we were truly lucky and blessed that nothing went awry. I had yet to take the basic, free boating safety course offered by the Coast Guard and my confidence far exceeded my good judgment. The only operating instrument on the boat was a compass. There were no cell phones at that time, and the boat had no ship-to-shore radio or depth finder. These are an absolute must-have for any craft. Radar, something else we didn't have, is also highly desirable as one crosses shipping lanes enroute to and from Catalina Island from Marina del Rey. Colliding with a huge container ship in the fog would be catastrophic.

Fortunately, the weather was kind to us, and using the compass and line of sight, we safely reached the shore of Catalina Island. We did have a chart, but were unable to determine exactly where we were. We spotted a nice sandy beach with beautiful, clear aquamarine water where several other boats were on moorings marked by large white floating buoys. Once again, we had no idea how to use moorings. Thankfully, other boaters assisted us with the process and we successfully moored *HIATUS II* to an available mooring in this incredibly beautiful cove which, we found out later, was Emerald Bay. A local harbor patrol boat later came by to approve and collect a nominal mooring fee.

We had safely arrived and filled with exhilaration, we cracked open a bottle of champagne to celebrate. The return trip two days later was, also, fortunately without any problems and we safely tied back up into my Marina del Rey slip.

The intensity of the experience and the associated wide range of feelings as one approaches and eventually reaches the relative tranquility and serenity of an anchorage or mooring are virtually impossible to adequately convey in words.

Only those of us boaters who have been there and done it can possibly relate.

It is a very gratifying and fulfilling experience, accompanied by an overwhelming sense of accomplishment. Having successfully traveled across the "high seas" with its waves, current, wind, and sometimes very challenging conditions, there is an enormous appreciation and gratitude at having made it to a safe harbor. You have challenged "Mother Nature" and won. As the "Captain of your ship" you have safely brought your vessel and passengers across the sea to a safe harbor.

The first time is perhaps the most vivid and intense; however, all subsequent "arrivals" also bring a wonderful sense of accomplishment and a feeling of inner peace.

As you approach your destination, you become busy identifying landmarks and checking latitude and longitude. Typically the wind drops, the sea flattens out, and the various signs of land ahead begin appearing. Seagulls circle above, kelp beds are visible below and around you. Sometimes inquisitive seals and other sea creatures are close by.

Finally, the anchoring or mooring process completes the arrival experience, followed by the inevitable ride to shore in your inflatable dinghy.

Over the next four years, I made countless trips to many Catalina Island destinations. My favorite was Twin Harbors (aka The Isthmus) where we had many memorable times. Unlike Avalon, a small town, the

Isthmus has only one small hotel, an open-air bar, a restaurant, and a provisions store. As such, the only visitors are fellow yachtsmen or daily visitors by ferryboats. This makes for a very friendly, party setting, so a good time is had by all.

During the four years that *HIATUS II* became my home, I had limited shared custody of my son Jeremy who, at the time, lived with his mother in San Diego. Every other weekend on Friday evening, I would pick up my son from Union Train Station in downtown Los Angeles, dedicate the weekend to a "Father-Son" experience, and return him back to the train station on Sunday evening. We shared some great times together. He quickly adapted to the life on a dock, had his own "Dinghy," became an avid fisherman, and accompanied me on many trips to Catalina Island.

2 OVER THREE DECADES LATER

HIATUS IV

HIATUS IV

1990 Carver Santego 38 Offshore Cruiser

- Length Overall 44'
- Beam 14'
- Twin 450 Cubic inch Gasoline Crusader Engines 350HP each
- Kohler Generator

Dining Area

Bar and Galley

Main Salon

This craft spent most of its life in freshwater in a covered slip. Sheltered from the weather and spared from the ravages of a saltwater environment, it has aged gracefully.

With good care from prior owners, this model of Carver was the last year that had extensive internal teak woodwork. For its relatively small size, this vessel, with a 14-foot beam, has a spacious interior, making it a very comfortable live-aboard.

ANTHONY ALCOCK

SECOND TIME 34 YEARS LATER

We now move the clock ahead some 34 years for my second experience of living on a boat. At the time of this writing, over two years have gone by since I, once again, became a "Live-aboard." A personally crippling financial venture involving the publication of a health magazine, combined with the collapse of my fourth marriage, led to the loss of most of my life savings, my home, most of my furnishings, and the humiliation of going through personal bankruptcy. For a while, I relocated to Europe and lived both in England and Spain, eventually returning to Southern California where, after much introspection, I decided to once again explore the live-aboard option.

While attending a boat show in 1988, I was really impressed with Carver's introduction of their 38-foot Santego model. I was so taken by the design and layout that, for many years, as a landlubber, I kept a promotional picture of this beauty on the wall of my home office. The aesthetically appealing design with careful use of internal teak cabinetry, doors, and accents make for a very spacious, essentially one-level vessel to comfortably accommodate, as guests, six to eight people. In addition, the relatively low-profile bridge has seating for twelve! The Santego is a great party boat and makes for a perfect live-aboard.

So, I decided to narrow my search for my new "home-to-be" to a Carver 38 Santego Model manufactured in 1988, 1989, or 1990, as these first three years were the only models that had extensive, decorative, internal teak. The internal fittings of subsequent Santego models, in the years 1991 and after, had a lot of bland, unattractive beige plastic, presumably because teak became scarce and prohibitively expensive.

Working with several yacht brokers, I looked at many potential options, none of which seemed to measure up to my expectations. Eventually, I located a couple of craft in the Sacramento Delta in Northern California. One in particular looked so attractive that I made a conditional offer and set off on the 400 mile drive north to go see it. This vessel is a 1990 model and had spent its life in freshwater in an undercover slip. As soon as I saw it, I was sold. The boat had aged well over its 24 years, thanks to the freshwater and protected slip that had been its home.

The usual sea trial and requisite boat surveys were performed and further negotiation with the seller took place, in order to compensate or fix a few problems that were uncovered. The sale was finalized and arrangements made to ship the boat by road to Southern California, a distance of some 400 miles.

Shipping loads that exceed certain width and height limitations require special shipping arrangements. Height cannot exceed 15.5 feet, and widths over 12 feet need a front and trail car with appropriate "Wide Load" signage. My Carver is 44 feet in length and 20 feet tall (Top of Navigation light to keel) with a 14-foot beam (width). So, in order to ship by road, it was necessary to completely disassemble the radar arch and Bimini top.

In hindsight, I should have supervised this process, which, at considerable cost, was performed by the boatyard in Stockton. There are, or should I say were, some 25+ wires and cables that snaked their way through the inside of the fiberglass radar arch to power the radar, autopilot, navigation lights, and a myriad of other things. My instructions to carefully label all wires that needed to be cut or disconnected were completely ignored. When it came time to re-assemble the radar arch at its new home in Ventura, it was virtually impossible to untangle the rat's nest of severed wires, resulting in significant expense to rewire everything. In total, this whole process of disassembly, shipment, re-assembly, and rewiring cost in excess of $7,000. Sad to say, the lesson here is to be careful who you trust in the "boating service" world and make sure that you over-supervise everything. After a week or so in the boatyard here in the Ventura Harbor, she was put back together, lowered back into the water, and has since been my home.

I renamed her *HIATUS IV*, as this seemed appropriate, representing "Time Out" after the collapse of my fourth marriage.

Ventura Harbor, the current home for my boat, is located 75 miles NW of downtown Los Angeles and has five marinas with 1,500 boat slips.

The Ventura Harbor Port District, home to the Channel Islands National Park, provides a safe and navigable harbor and a seaside destination that benefits residents, visitors, fishermen, and boaters. It has a quaint village with shops and restaurants and many weekend activities including entertainment, car shows, art events, and many different fetes.

Surprisingly, quaint Ventura Harbor is the second largest fishing port on the West Coast of the US (Alaska is the largest). Over 80% of the catch are squid, which are packaged and flash-frozen, with most of it shipped to Asia! The hive of activity with some 150 fishing boats and over 100 huge refrigerated trucks is carefully managed with a skill comparable to air traffic control. This is done so efficiently that it is almost transparent to the many visitors to the quaint village, which is an integral part of Ventura Harbor. This harbor brings in some 40,000 tons of fish per year, some 80% of which is squid, with an export value of around $50 million. Just one large "Seiner" fishing boat can hold up to 120 tons, usually caught in one trip of a day or so. Squid sells for about $650 per ton, so a full load can bring the captain close to $80,000! Of course, not all runs are full loads and there are a lot of expenses incurred.

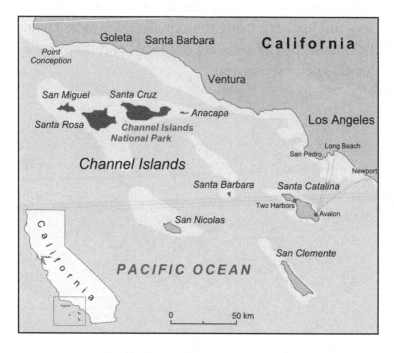

The islands off the coast of Southern California

3 | ADVENTURES ON THE HIGH SEAS

ANTHONY ALCOCK

ADVENTURES ON THE HIGH SEAS

PERSONAL EXPERIENCES

For most people who choose this lifestyle, the ability to drop the lines and take their home with them to other destinations is a high priority. Others, who live in houseboats or pseudo houseboats, still enjoy their home on the water and never move their craft from its slip or mooring.

For those who do take their boats out, there is a wide variance. Some are content to putter around a harbor or inland waterway, maybe tying up to guest slips at nearby restaurants. Others set off on world cruises. Most are happy to take a cruise on the ocean, perhaps to nearby islands, of which there are several off the Southern California coast.

Santa Catalina Island is a favorite destination for Southern California boaters. A rocky island off the coast of California, it is 22 miles long and 8 miles across at its greatest width. The island is located about 22 miles south-southwest of Los Angeles, California. The highest point on the island is 2,097 feet. Santa Catalina is part of the Channel Islands of California archipelago and lies within Los Angeles County. It was originally settled by Native Americans who called the island *Pimugna* or *Pimu* and referred to themselves as

Pimugnans or *Pimuvit*. The first Europeans to arrive on Catalina claimed it for the Spanish Empire. Over the years, territorial claims to the island transferred to Mexico and then to the United States. During this time, the island was sporadically used for smuggling, otter hunting, and gold-digging, before successfully being developed into a tourist destination by chewing gum magnate William Wrigley, Jr. beginning in the 1920s. Since the 1970s, most of the island has been administered by the Catalina Island Conservancy. The total population is approximately 5,000 people, 90 percent of whom live in the island's only incorporated city, Avalon. The second center of population is the unincorporated village of Two Harbors at the island's isthmus. Development also occurs at the smaller settlements of *Rancho Escondido* and *Middle Ranch*. The remaining population is scattered over the island between the two population centers.

Channel Islands National Park is a United States national park that consists of five of the eight Channel Islands off the coast of California, in the Pacific Ocean. Although the islands are close to the shore of densely populated Southern California, their isolation has left them relatively undeveloped. The park covers 249,561 acres, of which 79,019 acres are owned by the federal government. The Nature Conservancy owns and manages 76% of Santa Cruz Island, the largest island in the park. Channel Islands National Park is home to a wide variety of significant natural and cultural resources. It was designated a US National Monument on April 26, 1938, and a National Biosphere Reserve in 1976. It was promoted to a National Park on March 5, 1980. Channel Islands National Marine Sanctuary encompasses the waters six nautical miles around Channel Islands National Park.

I have personally taken many trips to Catalina Island, most of them to The Isthmus or Catalina Harbor. Almost all have been truly enjoyable and memorable. I have also anchored in many of the coves all around Santa Cruz Island. Catalina, for the most part, is "party time," whereas the Channel Islands offer many opportunities to escape to secluded coves where the water is unbelievably pristine and sea life is abundant. When anchored in one of these coves, it is is hard to believe that only twenty or so miles away is a mainland, home to some 25 million people!

There is abundant sea life in this part of the world. The Pacific gray whales pass by on their migration from the Bering Sea to Mexico (a journey of over 6,000 miles). Blue and humpback whales can also occasionally be seen. Pods of dolphins, sometimes as many as two hundred in a pod, are frequently seen when enroute to the islands. Often they will swim adjacent to the bow of the boat with amazing agility and speed. Others will surf behind you in the stern waves caused by your boat. There are, of course, many other forms of sea life, such as sharks, sea lions, seals, sunfish, and a wide variety of other fish. For the most part, these trips to and from the offshore islands are simply magical experiences and full of joyful memories. Following is a brief recount of my best ever boating experience, followed by a few inevitable "misadventures."

BEST BOATING EXPERIENCE EVER

Without question, the most amazing and memorable experience I have ever had was enroute to Anacapa Island from Ventura. The ocean is very rarely calm in these waters. A typical day has two- to three-foot swells, with an accompanying wind that makes visibility below the surface almost zero. On this particular day, one of only a couple that I recall in all my trips across this channel, there was literally no wind and the sea was flat and glassy, giving us some 100+ feet of visiblity below. I spotted a whale's spout (a whale exhaling through its blowhole) some 1/4 mile away. I immediately changed course and headed in that general direction. Within a few minutes, we were presented with the most spectacular sight, thanks to our very fortunate timing and the rare tranquil sea conditions. Only some fifty or so yards ahead of us, and about fifteen feet below the surface, stretched broadside across our path, was a female blue whale and her baby. I immediately halted our forward movement and put our engines in neutral.

The most magnificent sight lay before us; the largest living creature on the planet, some 120 feet in length (close to three times the size of my boat) with her 25-foot "baby" alongside her. Bright blue, in crystal clear water, this image will forever remain in my memory. We excitedly ran to the bow rail, where we stared mesmerized for several minutes before they slowly swam away. We were so mesmerized that we didn't even take photographs.

A FEW "MISADVENTURES"

"Now then, Pooh," said Christopher Robin, "Where's your boat?"

"I ought to say," explained Pooh as they walked down to the shore of the island, "that it isn't just an ordinary sort of boat. Sometimes it's a Boat, and sometimes it's more of an Accident. It all depends."

"Depends on what?"

"On whether I'm on the top of it or underneath it."

A.A. Milne, Winnie-the-Pooh

Occasionally, things don't always go just the way you would like them to go; after all, you are dealing with Mother Nature. Following are a few of my "misadventures."

THE DIABLO ANCHORAGE

As with all adventures, one inevitably experiences a few "bad trips." On one occasion, when attempting to anchor in one of the coves on the north side of Santa Cruz Island, we were preempted for the anchorage (Little Ladies Harbor) that was our original plan, because it was occupied and full. It was late afternoon and the seas were picking up, so we selected Diablo Harbor as our second choice. This anchorage is aptly named ("Devil" in Spanish). We double-anchored (both bow and stern) "by the book" adjacent to a cliff at what seemed to be a respectable distance. After an hour or so, both high winds and strong currents pushed us sideways dangerously close to the cliffs. With both bow and stern lines under heavy tension, it was increasingly impossible to shorten them in order to pull us away from the cliff, to which we were getting dangerously close. To compound matters, the bow line jumped the bow roller, which eliminated that option. I started the engines in the hope of carefully manipulating us out of our increasingly dire situation. We were, in fact, making some progress when our real nightmare began; the stern line got wrapped around the port propeller. We were now physically fending off from being smashed into the cliff with boat poles. I called SOS over our ship-to-shore radio and reached the Coast Guard. They were far away, however, fortunately, a large dive boat was close by and came to our rescue just in the nick of time. They entered the Diablo anchorage, threw us a line, and pulled us away from the cliff. They were forced to sever our anchor lines before towing us out into clear water. One of their divers cut away the remains of the stern line that had entangled our port propeller. Fortunately, we found out that we had not damaged the propeller or propshaft.

We thanked them profusely but now, with no anchors, had no choice but to return to our home port, Ventura Harbor, in heavy six- to eight-foot following seas. (A following sea is when one is traveling with the direction of the waves.) With a small power vessel, this can be very dangerous, as the waves pick up the rear end, causing the boat to "surf." One little wrong turn, and your craft will broach (turn sideways to the waves) and will, most likely, capsize. We battled this situation for the 20-mile return trip back to Ventura with numerous close calls where the boat lost steerage and came close to broaching. Fortunately, we made it safely back to the harbor. Several weeks later, I discovered that one of the divers on the dive boat that had saved us, based out of Santa Barbara, had retrieved our anchors. I drove up to get them and compensated them generously for saving our vessel and maybe our lives.

STORMY RETURN

I have had numerous, very pleasurable trips to and from the island of Santa Catalina. This was not one of them. We had spent several wonderful days on a mooring at The Isthmus, Catalina. Our plans were to return that Sunday, as we had business commitments beginning the ensuing week. The weather forecast was not good but, instead of using good sense, we decided to make the 68-mile trip anyway. After all, how bad could it get? Well, after only some 15 plus miles, it got very stormy and we found ourselves going head on into ten-foot seas. This is not comfortable in large vessels but, in small craft, it is downright scary. Turning back was not an option, as we would be in following seas and risk broaching and capsizing, so we battled on. Our speed had to be reduced to about 5-6 knots. as we were burying the bow and crashing back down over the waves that were coming toward us. With some 50 miles to go, this clearly was going to be a long trip!

I contacted the Coast Guard and we kept in touch every 15 minutes so that they would know our position. My crew was of no help, as violent sea sickness set in. I considered turning right to head to Marina del Rey, which was only some 20 miles away, however that meant the waves would be hitting our portside. This would be extremely dangerous, as we would likely be capsized by these huge waves.

With no obvious alternatives, I battled the remaining 50 miles for the next ten plus hours before literally "surfing" into the safety of Ventura Harbor. This was not a trip I wish to repeat. After this, I was very mindful of the weather forecast.

LOST IN THE FOG

If you anticipate fog or any other limited visibility conditions, you must have a working radar sytem and know how to use it. GPS systems today are quite powerful, easy to use, relatively inexpensive, and will tell you where you are. However, to avoid colliding with any other vessel or floating object, you need radar.

There are shipping lanes off the coast of Southern California and they run down between the coast and the offshore islands. The tankers and container ships that use these lanes are enormous. They travel at speeds of 30+ knots and, even if they see you, they are incapable of any rapid changes in course to avoid hitting you. You do not want to collide with these vessels. Radar will alert you to any vessel within close proximity and allow you to act accordingly.

During my earlier years of boating, I was embarassingly naïve, particularly regarding safety and the numerous potential dangers that are out there on the ocean. One day, in heavy fog with less than 30 yards visibility, the steel wall of a passing container ship suddenly appeared in front of us. I was able to rapidly change course and avoided colliding by only a few feet. On a diffferent occasion, two friends and I were returning to Marina del Rey from Catalina Island when we hit heavy fog. The direct course passes close by Palos Verdes Penninsula, a large headland that juts out into the Pacific Ocean. Absent any radar, but reasonably on course, we struggled to see ahead of us with very limited visibility. Unfortunately, the wind and current took us off course in an easterly direction. The sudden appearance of several small white buoys, used to mark the presence of lobster pots, gave us our first indication that all was not right. Suddenly, looming out of the fog, less than 100 feet in front of us, were waves crashing onto huge rocks at the base of this massive cliff. With great risk of damaging the boat's transmissions (drive trains), I throttled back, put the controls into reverse, and gave it full power. Fortunately, the engines and transmissions held together as we backed away. Eventually, I turned the boat around and headed in the opposite direction until we were able to recalculate a safer course. We had been seconds away from crashing onto that rocky shore! Once again, we were very fortunate to escape, and vividly reminded of the need for, and importance of, radar. Shortly after this, I installed both radar and GPS. A good depth finder is also a valuable instrument to alert you if, and when, you find yourself in shallow water, and you will.

DEALING WITH HEAVY SEAS

Back in the late seventies, while living on *HIATUS II*, I had taken my parents, who were visiting from England, on a trip to the island of Catalina. Also accompanying me was my current lady friend, Connie and my eight-year-old son Jeremy. The journey over was calm and a beautiful experience for all. We spent several days in Catalina Harbor on the west side of Twin Harbors. It was a magical time for all. However, nature will take its course and, just before our planned departure, the weather turned very nasty. I arranged for my parents and son to be transferred back to the mainland by helicopter, and Connie and I agreed to make the foreboding trip back up the west side of Catalina and on to our home port of Marina del Rey. In all fairness, I really don't think that Connie had any concept of the challenges ahead, and, in all honesty, I also was unprepared for the "battle" ahead to return to home port. As we all know, ignorance is bliss. After the safe departure by helicopter of my parents and son, we set off, with some trepidation, on our journey home. Frankly, in hindsight, it was very foolish to depart under these weather conditions. However, thanks primarily to my very seaworthy Chris-Craft lapstrake boat, we were able to survive 10- to 12-foot seas head on. It was a humbling experience to say the least and, certainly not one I would recommend. Burying the nose of *HIATUS II* beneath the oncoming waves was more than scary, but she held up and somehow we fought our way home. Cold, wet, and exhausted, some six hours later, we reached our home port in Marina del Rey. Alive and better for the experience, we kissed the ground (actually the dock) and told ourselves "Never again." It is very important to remember to respect "Mother Nature" because we are truly at her mercy.

GRAND LARCENY ON THE HIGH SEAS

Because of its absurdity, I felt that this "boating incident" was worthy of mention. Many years ago, a renowned ferryboat called the SS *Catalina* took people to and from the mainland and the Island of Catalina. By the late seventies, it had fallen into disrepair and its owner at that time had it anchored in the middle of Santa Monica Bay. Many curious visitors had boarded her and stripped her of anything of value so there she sat at anchor, a sad reminder of a once glorious ferryboat.

The year was 1979 and my children—a daughter aged fourteen and a son aged eight— and I were on a friend's high-powered inflatable dinghy out for a run across the Santa Monica Bay. We spotted the SS *Catalina* and motored in closer for a better look. Curiosity got the better of us and we decided to tie up our raft and go aboard for a better look. We had absolutely no intention of stealing anything, merely sight-seeing and showing my children the old SS *Catalina*. After seeing the sad state she was in, we spent no more than a few minutes on board. However, just before reboarding our inflatable, I spotted a book sticking out from a pile of trash on the ship's deck. Upon further examination, it was the engineer's log book. I thought, wow, what a find and how interesting this might be to peruse later, so I threw it into our inflatable dinghy and we set off to return home.

Unfortunately, some nosy, righteous people, who happened to be sailing by, called the Coast Guard, who apprehended us. Of course, strictly speaking, we were not supposed to board the SS *Catalina*, much less remove anything from it. The California Coast Guard, not known to be the brightest agency around, decided that we were hardened criminals. They arrested all four of us and put us, including my fourteen-year-old daughter, in handcuffs, while scaring the daylights out of my eight-year-old son! They took us into custody, impounded our inflatable dinghy, and charged us with "Grand Larceny on the High Seas." Relatives were contacted to take my children, while my friend and I were transferred to the local police, who threw us into a jail in Compton. Our bail was set at $10,000.00 each. Fortunately, our one permissible telephone call enabled us to reach our Israeli boat neighbors who came to our rescue with huge wads of cash to bail us out. However, the interim six hours in jail was not the most pleasant experience. Not surprisingly, the following day, we were informed that the current owner of the SS *Catalina* had no desire to press charges. So much for our beloved Coast Guard!

4 ALL ABOUT BOATS

ANTHONY ALCOCK

SELECTING THE RIGHT KIND OF FLOATING HOME

Boats come in all shapes and sizes and are designed for specific purposes. The choice for you is very personal and depends on your lifestyle. Living aboard gives one a certain independence and freedom but, at the same time, comes with a high price. Of course, much like the snail and his shell, all live-aboards have the option to move their home at will. This, in itself, is exciting, to be able to relocate all that you own (no packing) to a different location.

Boats are frequently referred to as she and her, and are often given female names. There is a reason for this. From a man's perspective, boats and women have a lot in common:

- Men derive a lot of pleasure from them in so many ways.

- They are high maintenance.

- It's exciting to take them to new places.

- They behave in ways that are frequently unpredictable.

- Men will go to great lengths and expense to make them look good.

- Men are proud of them and like to show them off to their friends and associates.

- They say that "The two happiest days in a man's life are the day he buys his boat and the day he sells it." Perhaps the same can be said for wives!

So let's briefly look at different types of floating homes:

BARGES (CANAL BOATS)

Barges were originally used to transport wood, coal, and other heavy stuff, and were pulled by horse at a slow but very steady pace. Later, small engines were installed to replace the horses. Transportation by barges was eventually phased out and replaced by trains and trucking. Canal boats were built with thick steel hulls and, because of the relatively narrow canals, they had a maximum width of about seven feet, but were as long as 75 feet.

Many of these old canal boats today have been converted into pleasure craft for hire and also make good live-aboard craft. Many European countries have kept and maintained their network of canals, providing the "canal boat live-aboard" with the opportunity to explore hundreds of miles of magnificent scenery without leaving home!

Certain inland waterways, rivers, and lakes can accomodate much larger and wider "barges," but this may limit where you choose to live.

HOUSEBOATS

These are found on lakes or sheltered harbors and, in general, tend to stay in the same place. They can even be multi-story and, as long as they stay afloat, there are no worries about sea-worthiness.

POWERBOATS

They can be as small as an inflatable with an outboard motor or as large as cruise ships and cargo vessels. For living aboard, anything smaller than a 30-foot craft is a bit confining. This means that it will probably be too large to tow on the highway on a regular basis and therefore will need a place to be moored, usually a slip in a boat marina or on a lake somewhere. Being permanently at anchor gets to be a real challenge going to and from shore. In general, for the same length (footage bow to stern), powerboats provide the live-aboard with much more living space than sailing vessels. Again, in general, most powerboats are not designed for long distance travel. They use too much fuel and therefore have limited range and are expensive to operate, except for short cruises. The exception are trawlers, which typically have single small diesel engines designed for longer distance travel at more affordable cost, albeit at slow speed.

Typically, offshore cruisers or trawlers afford one the most living space. There are multihull powerboats (aka power catamarans and trimarans) that also offer good living space, but they usually have a wider beam which may limit where they can be docked.

SAILBOATS

These come in many varieties and attract the nomadic, vagabond owners who often have dreams of adventure on the high seas. Most sailboats have a single hull with a center keel for stability. Others have either two hulls (catamarans) or three hulls (trimarans). Multihull craft typically afford a little more living space. Depending upon the number of masts and placement of the pilot station, sailboats have different categories: Ketch, Yawl, Schooner, etc. Earlier sailing vessels were "Square Riggers."

In truth, many sailboat live-aboards never leave their place of mooring. Those who do quickly become expert sailors, and are eager to share their experiences with those willing to listen; usually other sailors. It is not unusual for sailboat owners to regard powerboat owners with a degree of disdain (those "stink-potters"). Traditional mono-hull sailboats can be quite challenging to live on, unless one is fairly agile and comfortable with living in somewhat confined spaces.

DECIDING WHERE YOU SHOULD PUT IT

This really depends upon where you want to live. Maybe you want to cruise the world, in which case your "home base" is merely where you provision your boat before embarking and maybe a place to return. More likely, for most of us, you will select a home port from which you may go on trips to nearby islands or other anchorages of appeal. A large percentage of those who decide to live aboard never take their boats out of their slip! The marina becomes their home and neighborhood. In making this decision, here are some considerations:

- **Family** – Being geographically close to your kin may well limit your choice

- **Climate** – Given the option, one should choose a year-round warm climate as boats can become cold, damp, and uncomfortable in inclement weather

- **Cost of Slip or Mooring** – These can vary widely. An out of the way waterway or lake may cost little or even be free; however, unless you truly seek isolation, a marina designed to accommodate many boats is probably your best choice. Typically, marinas provide good security and basic services such as dockside bathrooms, laundry, and often a common boater's lounge. They charge a monthly rental that is based upon the length of the craft, usually a cost per foot plus an additional fee for the privilege of living aboard. Freshwater is almost always provided at no charge and electricity is metered.

- **Your Neighbors** – Marinas have differing rules regarding living aboard. Some do not allow any, whereas others set a maximum percentage. Having a lot of other people around you that also live aboard can bring mixed blessings. Boaters in general are a tight knit community and tend to watch out for each other, so that a high percentage of live-aboards usually means better security from potential thieves and a really nice sense of community. However, not all boat dwellers are quiet and respectful so, before committing, try to check out your new potential neighborhood for any "trailer trash."

- **Your Neighborhood** – Most marinas are in harbors that have a wide spectrum of services, shops, restaurants, activities, and entertainment. Check these out carefully to ensure that this is where you want to be.

Personal Note: I currently live in Ventura Harbor, a marina of some 400 boats with 50% of them live-aboards. This harbor, on the ocean in Southern California, enjoys a comfortably warm year-round climate and has a large tourist appeal with its many shops, arcades, and restaurants. It is also in close proximity to the City of Ventura.

5 | KEEPING YOUR BOAT AFLOAT

ANTHONY ALCOCK

THINGS TO CONSIDER

COST

There are several catch-phrases that aptly describe the cost of boat ownership. Among these are:

"BOAT = Break Out Another Thousand." Alex Blackwell

Other phrases include "A boat is a hole in the water into which you pour money." Unfortunately, as any boat owner will attest, boats require a lot of ongoing attention and maintenance, which explains the rapid depreciation in value of most watercraft. On or near the ocean, problems are worse, as a saltwater environment takes its toll on everything. Even stainless steel isn't stainless.

Unless you have reasonable D.I.Y. (Do It Yourself) skills, or deep pockets, don't buy, let alone live, on a boat. Even if you are capable of much of the maintenance, one quickly finds out that almost any fitting or part that needs replacement on a boat will cost two to three times that of a similar one for non-marine usage. There is some justification based upon the materials needed (bronze or stainless steel); however, if it goes on a boat, just expect to pay more. In general, the cost of a floating home will be considerably less than one on solid ground. However, with very few exceptions, boats are NOT an investment. Not only will you spend money to keep it afloat, but it will depreciate in value.

MOORING/SLIP FEES

Again, in general, the cost of living in a floating home will be much less than a home or an apartment. Typically, the marina, or whoever owns the waterway where you tie up your boat, will charge a monthly fee, often based upon the length of your craft. Mooring fees of $10-15 per foot per month, at the time of writing, are normal in a California marina. Inland lakes and waterways can be considerably less. Normally, an additional monthly fee is also added for the privilege of living aboard. This can be in the $120 to $300 range depending on the boat size and the number of people.

UTILITIES

Electricity is almost always available, metered for usage, and typically runs $30-60 per month. Water is almost always provided free of charge. "Grey water" (from wash basins and on-board showers) is typically pumped directly overboard. Sewage is macerated and stored in holding tanks aboard to be pumped out by special services or at pump stations set up for this purpose in the marina. Alternatively, one may pump out directly to the ocean once over three miles out from the coast. An alternative, depending upon the marina, is a mini on-board sewage treatment system that can be installed to pump the treated sewage (now technically grey water) directly overboard.

TAXES

Depending upon where you are, the governing authorities will typically assess you an annual tax just like a home tax, based upon the appraised value of your craft.

INSURANCE

This is not mandatory unless you are financing the purchase, however, I highly recommend obtaining full coverage. Of course, one always hopes that it will not happen to you; however remember, all that is important to you is in this floating bathtub, including possibly your family and pet(s). There are insurance companies who specialize in marine insurance and who often combine coverage for emergency towing, so remember:

- Your boat could sink due to an unexpected leak while you are away for only a few hours or even while you sleep!

- You could collide with another vessel or they could run into you.

- You could accidently run aground on a beach or, worse yet, on some rocks.

BOATING RULES AND REGULATIONS

When you find yourself piloting a floating vessel of any kind, whether in a harbor, on a lake, or on the ocean, you are subject to a whole new set of rules and regulations.

The sensible thing to do is to take advantage of the many free training and orientation classes that are available from the various local authorities. This can, and will, save you a lot of grief and potentially serious problems. I highly recommend that you take as many classes as you can. The old Boy Scouts motto "Be Prepared" is the way to go.

Being educated about boating before going out there is absolutely necessary. Ignorance is no excuse and water, especially the ocean, can be very unforgiving.

There are many basic rules that you must know before leaving the dock, for example:

- Basic navigation rules

- What to do in an emergency

- A checklist of requisite safety items such as location of life vests and how to use the radio and GPS

Even knowing all the rules, stuff can happen. When it does, and it will, the more knowledgeable you are, the better your chances of living to tell the tale.

In particular, the ocean can be very unpredictable and, when you are essentially alone on the ocean waves, you better be ready for whatever happens:

- Your engine(s) may fail.

- A calm ocean can quickly become a raging storm with enormous waves.

- A "Through-hull" fitting could break, flooding your vessel faster than any working bilge pumps can deal with it.

- You or a fellow passenger could become ill or accidently fall overboard.

These are but a few of the things that might happen. The point is, are you ready to deal with them?

SAFETY

"If you can't repair it, maybe it shouldn't be onboard."

Lin and Larry Pardey

Safety on a boat really includes being on top of many system checks and appropriate servicing. Here are some of the most important. They will vary depending upon the type of boat you have.

- Personal safety alarms - carbon monoxide alarms, smoke alarms, gasoline and propane vapor alarms. Press the test buttons, make sure the wires are connected, replace any batteries, and replace the units every five years

- Life jackets/PFDs (proper size, type, and stored in the proper location), flares (replace every 3.5 years), fire extinguishers (yearly inspection, five-year replacement or certification), horn, placards, and stickers

I highly recommend that you contact the local authorites, who are usually more than happy to give you guidance. There is no charge for theses services. If you are in an ocean marina, you will find the local coast guard very helpful.

MAINTENANCE

A boat (power or sail) is a very complex combination of electrical, electronic, mechanical, hydraulic, and plumbing bits and pieces. All of these must be operative in order for the boat to run and not sink. Regular maintenance and a watchful eye are imperative for one's safety and peace of mind. Again, the more one personally knows and can manage, the less one has problems and/or expense paid to others.

Boat plumbing is perhaps the most distasteful and difficult subsystem to manage. Leaks can cause the boat to sink or fill with fluids that you do not want in the bilges of your boat. The complex maze of pipes and hoses, leading to and from taps, showerheads, and toilets via holding tanks for both freshwater and sewage, can present one with some very unpleasant and odious challenges.

A couple of tips here: So called "Freshwater holding tanks" do not mean that the water is necessarily potable. The water may be fine for washing or showering or even acceptable once boiled, but after sitting in boat holding tanks and pumped through questionable boat plumbing, I would strongly recommend that, instead, one keeps bottled water on hand for drinking. Also, many craft provide an option for direct connection to water from the dock. While very convenient, one needs to be aware that any internal plumbing leak will cause the boat to fill up with water from the inside. Many boats have been lost this way. All boats have at least two or three bilge pumps to handle unexpected leaks of any kind, however, even if all are fully functioning, they probably will be unable to handle the volume produced by a high pressure deluge caused when a boat's internal plumbing fails while connected to an external city water supply. It is very important to check all bilge pumps on a regular basis and fix them immediately if they are not working. It is highly recommended that one turns off the external water supply at the dock whenever leaving the boat for any length of time.

A boat's electrical system may well present an even greater potential challenge. Most yachts, even small ones, have miles of wire of varying sizes and colors that are threaded through every accessible crevice and channel throughout the craft. Most of these wires are virtually inaccessible. The manufacturer's so-called "Operations Manual" will do little to explain this rat's nest of wiring. Typically, an older boat's prior owners will have added or changed the wiring for a variety of reasons so that it is not unusual to have switches and breakers that either don't work or do things that you didn't expect. To completely overhaul and rewire as necessary can be prohibitively expensive. As an example, on my current boat, *HIATUS IV*, there is a master control panel in the wall of the main salon that is divided into two sections: a 12 volt DC Power panel with some 32 breakers (switches that will also turn off if a circuit is overloaded) and a 110 volt AC Power panel with another dozen breakers, plus meters and controls for a generator, inverter, and battery charger. Not all these switches and breakers operate as one might expect because, over the years, changes and updates have been made. Behind these panels is a rat's nest of complex wiring that will challenge even the most experienced technician. In addition, the pilot station, which on my boat is on the flybridge, has many levers,

KEEPING YOUR BOAT AFLOAT

switches, meters, and controls to facilitate operating the craft. All of these have specific functions and need to be fully operational in order to safely move the craft from its slip, and get underway.

SERVICING

"If it doesn't move, and it should, use WD-40. If it moves, and it shouldn't, use duct tape."

Old Adage

- Service the engines, transmissions/drives (and generator), fluids and filters, spark plugs, and distributors (or injectors for diesel).

- Change the zinc anodes in the heat exchangers and coolers.

- Look carefully to see if you have any leaks – through-hull fittings, hoses, etc.Check gasoline or diesel for quality and fill tanks.

- Check and service rudder and propeller shaft seals. Repack traditional packing glands or service drip-less shaft seals.

- Service below waterline components, bottom paint, rudders, propellers, trim tabs, and bearings

- Check and service the engine's cooling system, raw water pump, impeller, and exhaust system. Again, check for leaks

SYSTEM CHECKS

- Check the shore power cord and inlet for heat damage, wear, and provide strain relief on the cord.

- Test and service the high water alarm.

- Check bilge pumps and automatic/float switches.

- Check batteries and cables for condition. Replace before they become a problem and ruin your next big trip.

CLEANING

Unfortunately, boats need a lot of cleaning. Much of this is not optional. Some or all of this can be done by the owner but, usually, is left to paid professionals.

It's truly amazing that, no matter what materials are used in the hull construction or what kind of anti-growth paint is used, tiny sea creatures will find a way to attach themselves to the bottom of your craft. Occasionally you can actually hear them at night while lying in bed. They have this faint but discernable clicking as they make themselves at home building a crusty film on the bottom surface of your vessel. Regular underwater cleaning of the boats hull is essential, especially in a saltwater environment. A monthly dive service to remove marine growth and replace zincs (See *Footnote*) as needed can cost around $2 per foot per month.

In addition, depending upon many factors, a haul out is recommended every two to four years. The boat is literally picked up out of the water with a powerful crane and placed on supports in a boatyard, where the full treatment can be performed on the underside of the craft. The hull is pressure washed, any defects repaired, and through-hull fittings are examined and replaced as necessary. Propellers and shafts are also cleaned and examined. A typical "Haul out" will cost $1,500 to $3,000.

Boats get dirty quickly, so the topside also needs regular cleaning (washing, soap scrubdown, and polish of stainless steel). Overnight condensation captures airborne dust and before you know it, it's time to wash the boat again. If you are young, full of energy, and have the time, count on a full soapy wash-down every two weeks or budget to pay a service to do it for you. Every two weeks is optimal and will cost upward of $200 per month for professional cleaning. The inside, just like a house, will also need regular attention and, although much smaller, often takes as much, if not more, effort.

In addition, boats typically have lots of "not so stainless" steel in the way of guardrails, radar arches, and the like, all of which require regular attention and special cleaning. Also, most of the surface area above the waterline is fiberglass and needs waxing every year or so, which is quite labor-intensive and time-consuming, or expensive if you pay someone to do it. If your boat has exterior exposed wood, it may look nice for a while, but can quickly become a regular time-consuming task to keep it looking good. Teak, now rare and expensive due to excessive de-forrestation, is one of the hardiest woods. It is resistant to salt water and used extensively for sailboat decks and other external wood fittings. Mahogany is also used externally on many craft. Regardless, all external wood on watercraft will need protection, sanding, oiling, or varnishing, and this will take lots of time and patience!

Footnote:

Zincs are sacrificial metal plates and collars that are attached to each and every important metal that is exposed to the water, such as propellers, drive shafts, trim tabs, and rudders. Electrolysis and galvanism will attack (eat away) the softest metal first. Zinc is a soft metal used for the purpose of saving the others. Different metals on a boat have differing electrical potentials. This electrical potential is called galvanism and is the reason why we put zincs on boats. Electrolysis is stray current escaping from the system and can be most damaging. When this happens, it will eat up the zincs in no time, usually leaving the zinc looking bright and shiny. Therefore: Shiny zincs = electrolysis. Dull eroded zincs = galvanism. Typically, zincs need replacing every few months depending upon the level of electrolysis in the water. The diver cleaning your boat will, for another fee, replace them as needed. You do not want to have to replace the propellers or other bits. Zincs are relatively cheap. There is also an internal bonding system which simply means that all the boat's underwater metals are wired together. This is done because of the galvanism caused by the different metals. By wiring them together, the differing potentials are equalized. This system needs to be checked to ensure that all connections are valid.

COMFORT

As the internal cubic feet of space in a boat is relatively small, keeping it at a comfortable temperature is relatively easy. Some craft come with built-in heating and air-conditioning systems. If this is not the case, there are numerous ceramic heaters or oil radiator heaters that work quite well and quickly get the boat to a comfortable temperature. In hot weather, open hatches and simple fans provide adequate cooling.

Because the lower 20% or so of your home sits below the waterline, even in dry climates, the humidity inside a boat will tend to be high. In some cases, this can present a number of challenges. Fabrics will smell musty, mold will collect and, in general, everything will take on that "boat smell." In addition, those prone to arthritis will get increased inflammation. Any "crunchy" food will quickly lose that characteristic. Crackers, cereal, and sugar lose their appeal in minutes.

There are ways to combat the ever-present humidity. Keep food in seal-proof containers. Install low-wattage heaters in all clothes lockers and drawers (piano or gun case heaters of 10-20 watts work extremely well). Leave these heaters on 24/7. You can also buy a dehumidifier unit. Keeping the boat well ventilated also helps.

Sleeping on a boat can be very pleasurable. The slight motion combined with the soothing sounds of a marina make for a sound sleep. Making the beds however can be quite an adventure, as sleeping quarters are often jammed into tight spaces. Learning how to make up one's bed, while standing in the middle of it, is a learned art.

6 CAPTAINS, WORLD CRUISERS, & VAGABONDS

ANTHONY ALCOCK

TRUE STORIES OF OTHERS WHO HAVE CHOSEN THIS LIFESTYLE

The boating live-aboard community attracts a wide spectrum of characters from wealthy vagabonds to trailer trash. There are masterful sailors, sea captains, "wanna-be sail around the world" types, loners, divorcees, and the list goes on. Some are "economically squeezed" for a variety of reasons. Most truly enjoy this choice of lifestyle. All have many things in common. They have all adapted to living in confined spaces, and most are eager to share and assist each other with the daily challenges of boat usage and maintenance.

In many ways, it is like a living soap opera. Occasionally it becomes annoying when those in the "trailer trash" category invade your space with their excessive noise and inappropriate behavior, but, fortunately, there tend to be very few of these. For the most part, live-aboards are very friendly and co-exist quite peacefully, so that, in general, marinas provide a very tranquil environment in which to live.

There are a surprising number of people that choose this lifestyle who are handicapped in some way or another. I had the honor to meet a very fit, middle-aged man who lost his eyesight at a young age. This man, a live-aboard, is an avid and very skilled sailor. Of course, he needs at least one crew member with full eyesight; however, those who have sailed with him told me that his sailing skills and "connection" with nature are truly remarkable. This chapter profiles the personal "live-aboard" true stories of several individuals and families who have chosen this lifestyle.

THE RIGNEYS

"January 2015 marked the beginning of a five-year round the world cruise for our family, an adventure we had been planning for some 16 years."

KANDU

1987 Tayana Vancouver 42

Center Cockpit Cutter

Tayana 42's are favored among circumnavigating couples and families for their safe, comfortable ride. Custom built in Taiwan, with added cruising amenities, this particular vessel spent half her life sailing the Pacific—Hawaii, Central America, South America, Polynesia, Melanesia, Micronesia, New Zealand, and Australia—and the other half in Southern California and the Sea of Cortez. The Rigneys purchased her for their intended circumnavigation, retrofitting all her systems including electronics, water maker, and plumbing. Additionally, they refinished the exterior and commissioned a hard dodger (a cover for the helm and instruments), and updated the amenities to include LED lighting and solar vents. With her wind generator, solar panels, water maker, and many redundancies, *Kandu* is a self-contained blue-water cruising vessel.

Forward Stateroom

Galley

CRUISING ROUND THE WORLD
ERIC & LESLIE RIGNEY

I am now in my mid-50's. My wife is in her mid-40's and we have two boys aged 11 and 13.

At age fourteen, I had my first sailing adventures as a young boy and decided that, once I could become reasonably financially stable, I would, with my family, embark on this ambitious and exciting adventure.

Main Salon

From that point on in my life, every serious, significant decision I made was influenced by my passionate intent to sail around the world.

In 1990, before we were married, Leslie and I sailed together around the Hawaiian Islands and back to the U.S. mainland on my uncle's 32-foot Ferro-cement boat to see if she shared my joy of sailing. She did, and we married some five years later on the mutual understanding that we would pursue our different careers and start a family, while saving enough to be able to finance our dream to sail around the world.

While not losing sight of our dream, I pursued a career in post-production with Sony Pictures for 20 years and my wife, Leslie, earned a PhD in music from UCLA and became a successful opera singer with the LA Opera for some 12 years.

We bought our boat, a 42' Tayana, on August 9th, 2010 (8/9/10!) in San Carlos, Mexico. My uncle, an avid sailor and boat builder, did extensive work on our boat here in Ventura.

The last two years really mark the commitment to "Just do it," and, for a while, we seriously considered a target of 70 countries while marketing to "TV Reality" shows. However, plans tend to morph and change, such that the goal is no longer to pass through as many countries as possible, but instead to circumnavigate while visiting more extensively specific countries of interest on our list. With that in mind, for our first year, we will head south to Mexico, obtain the requisite visas, and then head west across the Pacific Ocean to the Galapagos. From there we plan to go on to Easter Island, Pitcairn Island, and further west through French Polynesia. My Uncle Bill will also join us during our trip. To me, the value of having three generations cohabiting and sharing values and experiences in the close environment of a boat is very important

We are living and traveling on a boat as a means to an end. The "end," for us, is to expose our family to multiple cultures and also to introduce our children to multiple life skills, working together as a family. We will live shoulder to shoulder, learning how to deal with different people and cultures at each location we visit. Our two boys, aged 11 and 13, will learn, in detail, how all of the boat's systems function: engines, power generation, electrical, radio, communications, water making, plumbing, hull and rigging, etc., and how to fix them if they malfunction.

We also plan to document our experiences and adventures in a blog on our website www.rigneyskandu. com. In addition, we will post videos via YouTube at least weekly, if not more frequently. We will be able to closely monitor how our children learn and grow in this adventurous lifestyle, to influence more readily their likes, passions, and endeavors. What games will they play, high tech or otherwise?

Because we will have our own tightly controlled environment, we are essentially our own municipality, responsible for every system and subsystem that supports our floating home. We will share, as a family, all of life's challenges and opportunities both on our boat and wherever we go, exploring different places and cultures.

There is a slang term "Prepper" that people use to describe those who are preparing for an "End of the world" scenario. In essence, we are ready for that, though we are not expecting it! In our case it's not fear-based; we are just "prepared." On a boat, space is a real challenge. There is a delicate balance in terms of being prepared and carrying too much "stuff." While having spare parts and the wherewithal to fix anything is ideal, there is only so much room and time to prepare. It has been very cathartic to downsize and only keep a minimum of stuff.

We will be forced to work together in facing whatever challenges come our way, albeit natural forces or other. Nature is not personal. Synergistically working together, we look forward to addressing whatever "storms" come our way. We feel that this will bring a level of maturity to our children that would otherwise not be available. In today's society, with the possible exception of those raised in a farming community, children grow up with everything provided and little to want or strive for. Our children will learn to appreciate the basic needs for survival and self-sufficiency; no piped-in running water, no hot showers, no fast-food restaurants, no washing machines, etc. They will learn how to handle the tough times. Every project or activity, in general, takes 40% longer on a boat, simply because one has to pull stuff out, do the project, and then stow everything away again! My wife's biggest peeve is no dishwasher or clothes washing machine. Personally, I miss the large refrigerator and freezer and, of course, the large "workspace" of a garage.

The fact that on a boat there are so many systems and subsystems upon which we rely for our comfort and safety, although sometimes unnerving, does keep one alert and on one's toes and that's a good thing. I drive myself very hard because I don't just want to know which button does what, but what all is behind it and what the consequences are if it doesn't work and, most importantly, what I have to do to fix it.

Our boat is our house and home and we take it with us wherever we go. Some people enjoy cruise ships or fly to different destinations, but this is not the experience and adventure to which we aspire. This level of comfort anesthetizes and severely limits the experience. Being too comfortable deadens your senses. On a boat, your awareness level is heightened so that you are always conscious of the wind, the temperature, the sounds, the moon and all that is happening around you. We believe that this is the biggest gift we can give our children. By fully immersing them in this cruising experience, we believe that it will give them a solid foundation of skills and life experiences from which they can draw for the rest of their lives.

****

Track us on our Adventures @ www.rigneyskandu.com

THE ANDREOTTIS

"If God wanted us to sail, he wouldn't have invented motors."

POSEIDON

Hull – Fiberglass by Willard Boat Works

- Length Overall – 79 Feet
- Weight – 60 Tons
- Power – Two 545 HP CAT3406-B Turbo Diesels
- Transmissions – Two ZF V-Drives
- Generators – One 20KW Delco and One 8KW Northern Lights
- Inverter – 3,000W Heart
- Water Maker – 1,200 GPD Sea Recovery
- Fuel Capacity – 2,200 Gallons
- Water Capacity – 350 Gallons
- Beam – 20 Feet
- Draft – 5 Feet

Galley

State Room

JOHN & LINDA ANDREOTTI

MV (Motor Vessel) Poseidon is really the culmination of a lifelong search for the perfect floating platform. Her current home base is Ventura, California, a harbor ideally located to explore some of the most spectacular island anchorages to be found anywhere.

As a boy of ten in Sacramento, California, I remember how excited my two brothers and I would be when the rains started in early winter, because we knew that the drainage ditches, ponds, vacant lots, gravel mining pits, and any other surface depression would fill with water. If we were ingenious enough, and had scavenged the proper materials, we could build our watercraft and "sail" them to such exciting destinations as the Tree Groves where the pirates congregated, the deep gravel pits full of enemy submarines, the bushes of our neighbor whose darkness held crocodiles; and, of course, there were good people to be rescued. At the ages of fourteen, twelve, and ten, we were given an old rowboat that leaked despite all our patches. It sank in the ditch two houses down. Next, we decided to build a proper ship of great proportions, ten feet long, made of discarded potato sacks and old inner tubes. It sank too!

Later, with advice from my boss at the cabinet shop, where I worked the night shift cleaning the shop and building drawers, I learned more about boats and, in about seven months in Mama's basement, we built a twelve-foot long plywood catamaran. It was a remarkable piece of engineering, and quite pretty too. When we started to paint it, my brother Robert dropped the paint, which splattered the white primed boat with blue spots. We finished the paint job with intentionally thrown blue paint, and named it *I.C. Spots*. Now, when we could convince an adult to load *I.C. Spots* on top of a car, we would go fishing, frogging, and rowing in the nearby ditches and sloughs. We had no motor and didn't really understand sails, so we moved slowly but adventurously; saving maidens, finding treasures, and chasing away pirates and other scoundrels. Next we built a very usable runabout, scrounged an outboard motor, built a wooden trailer, and started cruising the rivers, lakes, and delta.

After, we built a succession of boats, each bigger and better, and all designed by me with my "helper brothers." There were race boats, ski boats, and more, but no sailboats. My favorite retort when asked why we didn't do sailboats was, tongue-in-cheek—"If God wanted us to sail, he wouldn't have invented motors." When Linda and I met and got married, we started to plan our ideal boat. In addition to seaworthiness, and all the practical aspects of boat design, we were determined to find, build, or develop a boat on which we could share our passion for food, wine, and the boating lifestyle.

Linda was, and is, the perfect partner for such an endeavor. She had previously owned and lived on boats – sailboats of all things! However, she quickly agreed that, for our dream of cooking, eating, and entertaining family and friends, we needed a larger boat with several must-haves. First, a great galley (kitchen); a spacious area overlooking the galley where friends and family could watch and participate; lots of storage for provisions of food, wine, and all the other supplies one needs for extended trips; a dining area for a dozen diners; a large outdoor cockpit for alfresco dining and entertaining; and of course all the comforts of a large home with guest accommodations. All of this had to be handled, operated, and maintained by the two of us.

It sounds easy, but it was not. After three years of searching, traveling all over the Pacific Coast, and frustrating yacht brokers, who told us that the boat we were looking for did not exist, and that we would have to build a custom boat to suit us and that it would be prohibitively expensive, we decided that one more try with a compromise boat would have to suffice. In desperation, we made a trip to San Diego to look at a converted commercial steel boat which turned out to be totally unacceptable. The broker we were talking to remembered another boat, which had been operated for years as a charter and corporate yacht and had recently been placed on the market. His opinion was that we were probably crazy enough to see that, in spite of her neglected condition, we could visualize the possibility of its return to glory and the fulfillment of our dream.

With sufficient apology, disclaimer, and head shaking, he introduced us to *Poseidon*. We walked down the ramp, saw Poseidon, stopped dead in our tracks, looked at each other, and knew that our prayers were answered. I said to Linda that, no matter how badly we wanted this boat, we could not appear too "sold." We needed to seem unconvinced so that we could negotiate the best price. We went aboard, briefly inspected her, asked a few questions, and Linda blurted out "We'll take it!" So much for seeming unconvinced! Probably somewhat half-heartedly, I tried to bargain. The price was too high. The boat needed too much work. She was too large for our needs. I brought up other objections, which I really did not believe because, I too, had fallen in love with *MV Poseidon*.

Having at last found our dream boat, we instructed the broker to get the deal done at a certain price, and threatened inhumane bodily damage if he didn't succeed. Naturally, he did.

We had fallen in love with *Poseidon* more or less as she was but, while all the mechanical systems were in an excellent state, our view of the interior and the layout quickly became jaded. No matter, we thought, love conquers all, and we began to make remodel plans and drawings even while the broker was doing his best to avoid injury and secure our dream.

Finally, the day came when we brought *Poseidon* to Ventura with the help of several of our friends. They all enjoyed the ride from San Diego, with an overnight stop at Catalina Island. I couldn't wait to start the rebirth of *Poseidon*, so much so that Linda had to stop me from initiating the remodel of the galley by tearing out the appliances while still underway. After all, she had ten people to feed and that is paramount to Linda.

As we approached Ventura Harbor, I rounded up the

whole crew to instruct them as to our landing procedure at the dock where I knew our friends, family, and dock neighbors were waiting, champagne in hand, to celebrate *Poseidon*'s arrival. My instructions were not quite as poetic as Nelson's.

"I have never docked as large a boat as this," I told them. "The marina has assigned us a very tight spot and, in addition, we have to back into the slip. So each of you fender handlers should stand by your assigned location, fender in hand, ready to ward off any potential collision! However there will be no yelling, panic, worried looks, or Chinese fire drills. Should we bump the dock, we will all act as if that was the plan." I believe there are two paramount boat rules: 'no yelling' and 'stay on the boat.' Yelling will turn the most idyllic voyage into a nightmare, as may a 'man overboard!' (I had, in fact, made two or three practice dockings in San Diego, which went quite well, but I wasn't going to admit that to the crew!)

And so we made our first Ventura Harbor mooring in the *MV Poseidon*. We did not hit or even touch the dock, much to Linda's relief. She had been quite nervous. As she stepped off the boat and wrapped a line on the cleat, a bunch of the boaters wanted to help her, but I calmly stated that Linda did not need any help. We two would complete the maneuvers, just as we would have to for as long as we cruise *Poseidon* and, to this day, we politely and appreciatively refuse all offers of assistance. When someone is kind enough to comment on how well we handle *Poseidon*, I tell them that the boat drives herself. Poseidon does indeed handle better than any other boat I have piloted.

The renewal of *Poseidon* started immediately and continued for about two years. 'The next few months' was our original expected term of all such work. How wrong can two boat owners be?

With plans drawn, budget prepared, lists made, and new tools at the ready, the demolition started. First priority was temporary sleeping accommodation, for we were going to live on the boat throughout the remodel. We chose the aftermost double cabin to sleep in and, of course, we had to have some sort of cooking facilities on board.

Fortunately, the aft stateroom, which was the largest on the boat, didn't require major modification. We added a closet, new mattress, a TV, and tore out what seemed like tons of excess equipment such as air-conditioning units, intercoms, required Coast Guard signage and emergency gear. (Previously, Poseidon was Coast Guard certified to carry 49 passengers for ocean work.)

Then I brought out the chain saws, wrecking bars, and other demolition tools. Linda insisted that I only work on one area at a time, so we started in the galley and salon area. Needless to say, the galley was the most important project of all. Nothing is more important to Linda than to be able to cook. It's hard to imagine how much wire, pipe, appliances, flooring, and other materials came out of a boat which at one point we thought would need only minor cosmetic work. The dock was constantly piled up with stuff which we hauled away as fast as we could with the help of our friends and a few hired hands. Fortunately, our fellow boaters are scroungers by nature and much of our junk ended up in other boats and dock boxes (no doubt to be thrown out when the scroungers realized that it was no more use to them than it was to us!).

The more you remove, the more you expand the project and we now found ourselves with bare walls and floors. 'Minor cosmetic work' turned into a complete rebuild. It was time to bring in all of the reinforcements I could assemble, namely ... Mama (my mother). I picked her up every morning and she worked all day with me. Sure enough, we started to see results. Now and then, Mama complained a little and I had to remind her that, years before, when she and Wayne decided to build a house themselves, despite their complete lack of experience, it was me who was the everyday helper. This, I said, was payback.

Actually, Mama enjoyed helping me and I really enjoyed having her with me. When Linda came home at the end of the day, Mama proudly showed her our progress. The projects became more and more ambitious and, with the galley functional, we would stop work a little early, open a bottle of wine, and Mama cooked. Friends and neighbors came in, ostensibly to inspect the work, but I think the real attraction was Mama's wonderful and authentic Italian cooking. We spent several happy, busy months working seven days a week in this manner and the results were beyond our wildest expectations. For further updates on "Life aboard *Poseidon*" and, in particular, Linda's Cooking, go to:

www.poseidoncooks.com

ANTHONY ALCOCK

THE EELLS

Life may be a 'Great Balancing Act,' but through it all
'There's fun to be done.'

Dr. Seuss

VALHALLA

> Length Overall 62' LOD 58', Beam 17'
> Engines: Single Perkins 3.54 L, 140HP (English)

This craft is a "Dynamique 62" built in the mid-1980s. It has an IOR hull designed by Phillipe Briand. The interior has been completely gutted then designed and rebuilt by the owners, Jonathan & Brenda Eells.

JONATHAN & BRENDA EELLS WITH THEIR CHILDREN SIDNEY, WYATT, & AUDREY

Born in Gatlinburg, Tennessee, I, Jonathan, literally, at the age of eight, broke into the boating world by skimming an oyster shell through the plate glass window of our local yacht club. It was not intentional, so I confessed and was actually commended for my honesty.

As a child, I gravitated to a ferry that ran across the Chesapeake Bay from Oxford to Bellevue. Captain Benson, who ran the boat, indulged me and I traveled to and fro across the bay. I loved it and, free of today's litigation and rules, I was permitted to do many tasks including taking the wheel. This was my first exposure to the boating world and I was "hooked." We moved a lot after that, my mother and I. She was an ex-Marine but not that "well," and so we did not stay put in one place for long. At one point, I counted 37 times in a matter of 13 years! My favorite places were those that had boats—Maine, Alaska and Florida.

At age 13, I finally abandoned my mother and moved into a foster home in Boulder, Colorado. I somehow found myself in college in Ohio, which is a great place to leave. I met my wife in Wyoming and she, raised in Ohio, also was glad to not be there.

For a while, we lived in a house on Lake Arrowhead up in the Los Angeles Mountains. I had a few boats up there, including a Lido 14, a rowboat, and an 18-foot Cape Dory "Typhoon." The Dory had this huge 900 lb. keel that gave it incredible stability. On Lake Arrowhead, winds of 30+ knots can appear out of nowhere and, as I had my young children sailing with me, safety was paramount.

After this, we started getting bigger boats. We got a 25-foot Pacific Seacraft Double-ender, manufactured right here in Ventura. We kept it in Dana Point Marina while still living on Lake Arrowhead. Our next acquisition was a Catalina 270 which, although quite spacious, my wife thought was not big enough. We then stumbled into a Robert Perry design "Panda 40." It's a full keel Hans Christian "knock-off" with a canoe stern, a beautiful teak bowsprit, and lots of other teak everywhere. Its name was *Valhalla*. At about this time, we had an awful forest fire at Lake Arrowhead which destroyed 160 homes. Ours, sheltered behind the crest of the hill, was spared, but this really woke us up to the reality that we could easily have lost all we owned and, according to the newscasts, at one point, thought we had! At the time, we were on our boat in Oceanside. Coincidentally, there was a fire at Camp Pendleton which rained ashes on us. We felt as though the whole world was on fire. Even though our home was spared, we realized our vulnerability up there at Lake Arrowhead. We decided to get a bigger craft and make it our home. What followed was the biggest "downsizing exercise" ever. We had collected lots of stuff and moving from a house to a boat forces you to drastically get rid of most of it. We literally filled up four dumpsters!

So we purchased our current boat. It was actually a race boat, but it will never race again. It had several previous owners and has sailed around the world. The prior owner made a real mess of the inside, so I have personally gutted and rebuilt it to meet the needs of our family, now my wife and I, our three children, and two cats. We had the luxury to rebuild the inside to our exact requirements. The project took some two years. I worked on it daily while we lived in Marina del Rey in an apartment overlooking the slip where she was tied up. Once I was finished, we moved on board and immediately set sail for San Francisco. Unfortunately, the San Francisco Bay is fairly shallow (around 16 feet) and with a draft of some 9 feet, it's a bit risky, unless you stay in the shipping channels. So, we also bought a Catalina 22 so that we could sail around and enjoy the bay area. We stayed for about a year, then put our name on a waiting list for here in Ventura. To our surprise, the anticipated wait time of 12 months turned out to be only five days, so we moved down here in late 2014.

Our goal is to live here and regularly sail to our local Channel Islands, where we can anchor, swim, hike, then sail home. My children love Ventura. We all love the city of Ventura and so this is our home.

One day, while in the engine room, I heard voices asking "where is Dad" and at that point I realized that if I could actually get "lost," this boat is big enough. Actually, each of us has our own cabin. I felt it important that each child have his/her own space, and they do. Also, we have a large main salon and large galley. I completely re-wired the whole boat. I pulled out over 1,000 lb. of old wiring! One of the smartest things I did was to become a member of the ABYC (American Boat & Yacht Council). It is like a standards organization that has developed, in great detail, how everything on a boat should be to conform.

My wife has an excellent job in civil engineering and can work from home a lot. I built her a desk in our own private cabin.

I act as "House Husband" and I love it. I actually stopped just short of a PhD in International Relations. I exited with a Master's Degree when I realized that I was not going to teach, so I left just before I submitted my dissertation. Part of my choice goes back to my childhood. I decided that I was going to be a really good parent and I truly enjoy it.

As to the future, it's really pretty open. We don't have too many fixed plans. We stay open-minded and keep our options open. I will complete the cosmetics on the rebuild and enjoy our life.

A favorite of mine is Dr. Seuss's wonderfully wise graduation speech for his own daughter. Dr. Seuss addresses life's ups and downs with "Life may be a 'Great Balancing Act,' but through it all 'There's fun to be done.'" He also stresses don't stay in "The waiting space"! We are here in Ventura and we enjoy it. We did join the Ventura Yacht Club and get involved in some of the more exciting activities for all of the family.

Like most boaters, we have had so many magical experiences. One of the most spectacular was very early one morning as the sun just arose behind me, I saw this meteor come blazing across the sky, a bright green color which then exploded. They are known as "Bullet Stars." Also, it is truly amazing, on crystal clear nights, to look up and see the Milky Way and a sky full of so many stars. To non-boaters it is impossible to explain so many of these experiences that landlubbers will never see.

ROUILLARD & HUBER

"All in all, life is good....Especially the second time around."

PACIFIC HARMONY

1984 Californian 43 Cockpit Motor Yacht Specifications

- Overall Length: 46'
- Beam: 13'
- Power: (2) Caterpillar 302 HP Diesel engines
- Genset: 7.7 kw, Westerbeke diesel
- Flybridge control station
- (2) heads complete with showers
- Step Down Galley

- Forward V Berth, and Aft Master Berth
- Full Raymarine Navionics
- Radar, Autopilot
- Satellite TV Antennae system
- Enclosed Sundeck

MARY LEE HUBER AND JERRY ROUILLARD

Jerry is a USCG 100 Ton Master, American Sailing Association Certified Instructor, a commercial aircraft pilot, and a United States Parachute Association licensed expert parachutist.

Mary Lee is a big band and jazz trio pianist and vocalist. A Wisconsin Music Education Association Master Adjudicator, she is also a recipient of numerous education awards.

Jerry and Mary originally met in the summer of 1967 when they were both working in Wisconsin Dells, a huge tourist destination. Jerry was a skydiver in the Tommy Bartlett Water Show and Mary Lee was a college senior singing and dancing in a hotel revue. After the summer employment was over, they went their separate ways, each with memories of a great summer relationship.

After thirty-one years, they reconnected and discovered that the long separation had only enhanced their original attraction. During those years, Jerry had many unique jobs in all parts of the country, and Mary Lee had found her niche as a music teacher. Each had acquired a Master's Degree in their respective fields. They both retired in 2004, Jerry as Museums Director in Placer County, California and Mary Lee from thirty-six years of junior high choral music teaching in Wisconsin.

A search for more sunshine in the winter months, combined with their love of sailing their Pearson 39 sailboat, found them heading to the warmer waters of Pacific Mexico for the next seven winters. La Paz was their home port for four of those years, and the Sea of Cortez was their favorite sailing destination.

After selling the sailboat in 2012 and buying the trawler, they now call Ventura, California their home port. The Channel Islands, just off the coast here in Ventura, make for great sailing destinations.

Pacific Harmony affords them room for Mary Lee to have a digital piano on board, the addition of rescue dog "Sula," and a walk-around bed! During the summer months, they return to Mary Lee's family farm in Wisconsin near St. Paul, Minneapolis, where they have a Catalina 25 sailboat that they sail on Lake Pepin, a wide spot in the Mississippi River near Mary Lee's family farm. There they also reconnect with family and friends (Jerry is originally from Anoka, Minnesota), and Mary continues to perform with the Generation II Big Band.

Living on a boat has many enjoyable aspects; waterfront accommodations, ease at changing neighborhoods, interesting wildlife, and a broad spectrum of interesting neighbors who are easy to meet and socialize with. There is also a sense of being more in touch with nature and the sea. Of course the need for space management automatically limits the acquisition of too much "stuff." However, boats are depreciating assets, can present challenges to those with health or mobility issues, and present a challenge to maintain the various complex marine systems. Perhaps one of the most exciting and interesting aspects of living on a boat is the ability to take your home to the adventure so you can live it instead of simply visiting it.

All in all, life is good....Especially the "Second Time Around."

ANTHONY ALCOCK

MEGAN ROGERS

"The bottom line is that I treat my boat as a floating condominium."

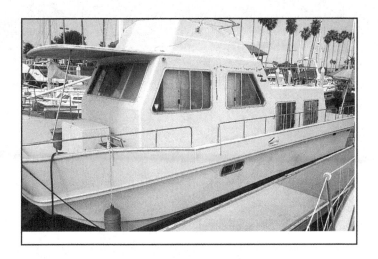

TICABOO

1989 Holiday Mansion "Barracuda"

This very spacious vessel makes for an ideal live-aboard craft, capable of sleeping up to four people.

' 1 Bedroom, 1 bathroom, Main Salon, and Galley
' Length 38', Beam 13'

ANTHONY ALCOCK

MEGAN ROGERS

Actually, as funny as it might sound, I have never been that interested in boats.

My mom has been sailing since I was a kid. My brother also got interested after my mother bought her first boat. However, sailboats and boating in general were not for me. The only reason that I moved on to my mom's sailboat was because when I left my "ex" (we were not married, but had a long exclusive relationship), I had nowhere to go at that time. We had been "living on the road" for a while. So, I split, moved my stuff out of the house that we almost never lived in anyway, and, with Mom's approval, went to live on her sailboat up in Washington State.

PyeWacket

Later, because a friend of mine was living down in Ventura, I decided to move her sailboat down there. I didn't sail it down; I shipped it down. I lived on it for about 18 months until I decided to start my own business in mobile food catering. My mother actually came down to help me get the business started. At that point, I decided to buy a houseboat, the one that I have now, which I have lived on, with my cat "PyeWacket," for the last two and a half years.

My mother, after a trip or so back up to Washington, also moved down here to Ventura and, today, lives on her sailboat across in the other marina here in Ventura.

I do like it here and, with my history of living in small

spaces, it works for me. For about four and a half years, we (my "ex" and I) lived "on the road" in a 27-foot truck, so I became accustomed to living in small spaces. We operated a mobile food truck, catering to music festivals of all kinds all over the country. We started in our cars, then the truck, and eventually bought property in Joshua Tree, California. We lived in the house for about six months, after which we went back on the road for about a year before we split up.

I do need to tell you that I hate sailing. Both my brother and mother are avid sailors but, the few times that I have been with them sailing, I hated it and was seasick. I just don't like sailing.

I do, however, love the water and really like my life living on my houseboat. It's not going anywhere. In fact, it's never been out of the slip, and that's OK.

Many people who live on a boat do so because they feel the need to change their lives and need to do some soul searching to "find themselves." They "downsize" to change and simplify their lives. That is not why I live on a boat. For me, it is a matter of survival. I first lived on my mother's boat, then moved to this one and it works just fine.

However, at this point in my life, I think I am ready to live in a real house with spaciousness, full-on long hot showers, and a garden.

If my personal relationships work out the way I would like, then, at some point, I look forward to a living in a house on land and I mean a house, not an apartment.

Perhaps the worst part of living aboard for me is the need to use the "dock facilities" for personal bodily functions. An acceptable toilet, full-on shower, and a large kitchen would be a real plus for me. A ten-minute shower would be wonderful.

I made the move to live on a boat because, at the time, financially, it was the right thing to do.

One of the highlights of living on a boat is that I just love the water. One of my favorite things to do is to sit on my back deck and enjoy the ambience of the marina. I see all kinds of birds, including pelicans and blue herons. I see harbor seals and the occasional dolphin that cruises by. I just love watching the birds. They are absolutely hilarious in that they play games with each other. They are so intentional, if that's the right word, in that they bait each other. For example, the other day, I watched a couple of seagulls on a light pole jostling each other, one trying to push the other off the edge. I love humming birds also.

The bottom line is that I treat my boat as a floating condominium. One of the surprising things about boats is that most people have no idea what the insides look like. When you step aboard my boat, it's my cozy home and I do love it.

THE CASSONS

"Overall, we have to say that boat life is wonderful."

NOSTRA TANA

46' Maxum LE Flybridge Motor Yacht

- Year Built – 2001
- OAL - 46'
- Beam – 14'
- Draft – 4'
- Engines – Twin Cummins Diesels 450 cu in.
- Weight – Gross 29 tons, Net 23 tons

Main Salon

JOHN & JENNIFER CASSON

We first met towards the end of 1991. John was born and raised in England and came to the U.S. in 1998. Jennifer was born in Poland and moved to the U.S. at age 16. We worked for a few very wealthy successful business people as "Estate Managers" since the early 1990s. When we first met, we bickered a lot, but I think we both knew that there was something special going on. Eventually, we grew closer and married in 1995. At that time, I had a small 28-foot Bayliner power craft, but Jennifer was not really into boating, so we got an apartment in Playa Del Rey.

Jennifer was always terrified of water. At age 10, she almost drowned in the Baltic Sea in Poland. As a result, she never thought that she could really get into the boating world, let alone live on a boat. She couldn't even swim! In 1997, we bought a house in the desert which had a pool and it was there that she learned how to swim for the first time and that helped a lot. I was very passionate about boats and, eventually, Jennifer came around and we started looking at them. At the time, we really hadn't thought about the possibility of actually living aboard. By the end of 2002, after looking at about 40 different boats, we bought a 43-foot Irwin Mark III, a sailboat. The main thing that we liked about her was her large stern cabin with this big bed and nice bathrooms. So we purchased it and moved it to Ensenada, Mexico for six months or so while we checked out other marinas in Southern California.

We fell in love with Ventura Harbor, especially Ventura West Marina Phase II, because the beach is right there and we just love the village, the people, and the area. At the time, we were working as estate managers for very wealthy people in the entertainment business, and we decided that Ventura was a perfect place to settle in. We had checked out Marina Del Rey, but found it much too congested and expensive, plus the commute would have involved heavy traffic. Initially, we had difficulty getting a "live-aboard" slip in Ventura, so we bought a house here and we were "Sneak-Aboards," spending a week or so on board, then staying at the house for the rest of the time.

We enjoyed many wonderful trips to Catalina Island and the Channel Islands. An old friend and business associate from some years ago named Adam Burkot, who was also of Polish heritage and an avid sailor, taught us how to sail a few times. On our first trip to Catalina Island, he and his wife went with us. For whatever reason, they had decided to go back and left, and we were faced with taking our boat back to Ventura on our own. On the way back, the weather turned pretty bad and we battled through our first challenging experience alone. The storm was awful, but the boat was very seaworthy and we made it safely back to port in Ventura. At one time, we spent almost a month in Catalina Harbor, which is on the western side. We almost grounded her when we first got there, as it gets shallow if you go in too far. However, we survived that experience.

In 2012, I had a pretty bad car accident and couldn't handle sailing anymore, so Jennifer and I decided to get a powerboat. We sold our sailboat but then, suddenly, the market changed. Boats were in high demand, and we had a hard time finding what we wanted at a price we could afford. We narrowed our search so that we were looking for a fifty-foot motor yacht in the $200,000 to $600,000 price range. The Italians had stopped exporting their craft, so it became a seller's market. We found only three boats that met our criteria. We found our current boat in San Diego. We almost bought a larger boat, a "Sealine T 50," but it was really too big and not quite as good a condition as the one we have now. We had kept and paid our slip for several months because we didn't want to lose this great location. We actually bought our current boat, *Nostra Tana*, in July 2014 and brought her from San Diego on my birthday, July 28th. Jennifer is still trying to perfect her captain's skills, but she is doing much better now. We just love this boat. Of course, like all boat owners, we hope that nothing major goes wrong because, as we all know, it can get expensive. The important thing is that we keep up with all the required maintenance. We do as much as we can and hire professionals to do the rest. When we bought the boat, the prior owner had really taken good care of it. It had cost about $500,000 when new in 2001, plus he had added about $100,000 worth of extras. When we purchased her, she only had some 300 hours of usage, which, of course, is very little. He was anal about everything, even putting absorbable "diapers" under the engines. It also has a $7,000 "flushing system" that I have yet to figure out!

Overall, we are really enjoying our life aboard. It is just the two of us and our African Grey parrot, "Fiji." We really love our Fiji. She has been with us for 18 years and, because they live some 80 years, we need to consider where she goes after we are gone. We know, of course, that a boat is not an investment, so we embrace the wonderful lifestyle of living here. Eventually, we plan to get a small but very comfortable motorhome so that we can occasionally take off and travel around the country. After living on a boat, you get accustomed to living in small spaces.

What we really like about living on a boat is the environment on the water and the friendly,

John and Fiji

down-to-earth people. We lived in Malibu for a long time and dealt with many pretentious, discourteous, and rude people who wouldn't lift a finger to help you. Even living in most houses or apartments, you often don't get to socialize with your neighbors. The boating community is unique in that everyone is friendly and cares about their neighbors. Also, if your business or other plans cause you to relocate, you can take your boat with you. It's great to take off to the islands for a few days and take your home with you. For quite a while, due to my role in business, I was almost invisible, as I was sometimes working or on call 24/7. They referred to me as the "Phantom."

One of the things that concern us on a boat is the ongoing maintenance, especially the unexpected large cost items. The birds, although nice to see and hear around us, do make a mess with their droppings. Of course there is always the possibility of an earthquake or a tsunami, which could be devastating for us all. One night, a large dive boat, with some drunken captain in control, ran into our boat here in the marina. It was early in the morning and we were literally knocked out of bed. I thought, 'This is it, we're going down!' The boat then careened off several other vessels, causing a lot of damage. Of course, these things don't happen often, so we try not to worry about them.

Our location, which is on an end slip, affords us many exciting visual experiences. As an example, we can see the boat ramp where they launch the smaller craft from towed trailers. We have seen cars, obviously with brakes not set right, get dragged back completely into the water by the boat being towed. We once saw a boat go by actually towing its own trailer. One day, this friend of ours was having his boat put back in the water by the boatyard (lowered in on straps by the crane) and they forgot to close the sea cocks, so the seawater rushed in and almost sunk his boat. Another day, this same man was motoring by on his sailboat, alone, and somehow, while messing with his mainsail, was suddenly pivoted out some ten or more feet dangling over the water while hanging desperately on to the mainsail boom. Fortunately, someone came to his aid and rescued him.

We plan to go to Catalina for a couple of weeks in the near future. It's expensive for the gasoline but, when you realize that it's also your hotel, it really is quite affordable.

Overall, we have to say that boat life is wonderful. The positive aspects far outweigh all the negative stuff.

ANTHONY ALCOCK

BEN GREEN

"All in all, however, I have to say that life on a canal boat is truly joyful."

IRRESPONSIBLE

1997 Narrow Boat

- Overall length 45' Width 7' 11"
- ½ inch steel hull
- Galley, lounge, one bedroom & bathroom
- BMC 1800 cc Diesel engine

My Lounge & Galley

BEN'S STORY

I first became interested in boats when, as a young kid, I went sailing with my Uncle Patrick. The experience, at the time, really grabbed me. I thoroughly enjoyed the whole sailing scene.

Later, after my dad died in 1997, a friend of mine, Toby, invited me to go sailing with him. Shortly after leaving, we were caught in a Force 9 gale in the Bristol Channel, in which Toby's girlfriend was very ill. We recovered and sailed down to Cariño on the north coast of Spain. Later, we went around Cape Finisterre, a rock-bound peninsula on the west coast of Galicia,

Spain, on our way to Vigo. Later we took a trip down to Porto in Portugal.

Upon returning to England, after these boating experiences, I thought, 'I just can't live in a house anymore.'

A mate of mine said he was going to the Canary Islands for a while and asked if I would be interested in taking care of his canal boat while he was away. I said yes and, after two weeks of living on and taking care of his boat, I was hooked. I no longer wanted to continue the business that my dad and I had run before he passed away. It was a car radio decoding business, whereby we were able to reactivate car radios for people who, for whatever reason, had lost the code number to key in to make the radio usable. My passion is, and has always been, more into landscape gardening. I'm very good at it and have done it for some fifteen years and I love it.

Anyway, my friend Toby called and invited me to join him in Portugal. So, I did this for about a year, and we had a great time. I rented out my own canal boat while I was away. It was in Portugal that I met my wife "Kat," who is an American. We migrated to Florida in the U.S., where we lived for about three years. I can't say that I liked Florida very much, so we came back to England and bought yet another canal boat.

Now, I know that I really couldn't live in a house. I don't want a letter box and people soliciting. I love the tranquility of living on a boat. We are a very close community, those of us that live on canal boats. We take care of each other and we share a lot in common. We often eat together with barbeques, right there on the towpath adjacent to where we tie up our boats.

Chandler

If I don't like where I'm at, I simply move my home somewhere else. I am my own man and I live a lovely life on the canal. Every two weeks, I move to a different spot. If I don't like my neighbors, I simply untie my ropes (lines) and move somewhere else. There are literally thousands of miles of canals in the UK. However, I usually stay within a twenty-mile radius. It's pretty easy really, as it's just me and my cat, Chandler. My wife and I parted some time ago. My cat is very special to me, though she does get aggressive occasionally. She often scratches me and is always chasing dogs.

There are some very special people in the canal boating community and some of them play an important role in my life. Our "community" consists of about 30 to 40 individuals from all different backgrounds. A few of them are quite unique. For example, we even

ANTHONY ALCOCK

have our token transvestite. It's an interesting mixture of characters that choose this lifestyle, but they are all good people.

I have actually lived on a canal boat now for about seventeen years, with some time out when I lived in Florida. However, I always kept a boat to come back to. Usually, I rented them while I was away.

The important thing here is that I always kept my Canal & River Trust "Continuous Cruising License," which enables me to not pay mooring fees, providing that I move every two weeks, which, in reality, makes life more interesting.

As to the future, I would love to travel through the extensive inland waterways of Europe.

There are, of course some challenges and annoyances with canal boat living. Probably the worst being the toilet, as one does need to empty it frequently and it's not the most fun thing to do!

All in all, however, I have to say that life on a canal boat is truly joyful.

THE BREWERS

*"In my opinion, there is nothing better than
the boating lifestyle."*

Photo by Dina Pelosi, 451 Media 853-641-4100

NIGHTHAWK

Formosa CC Ketch

Built for Sylvester Stallone in 1981 after he completed the film
Nighthawks

1980 Formosa CC Ketch Nighthawk

- Engine - Ford Lehman Diesel 80 HP
- LOA 55'
- LWL: 42'
- Beam: 13'10"
- Draft: 6'8"
- Mast Height: 55'
- Hull - fiberglass
- Water 200 gallons (stainless)
- Fuel: 225 gallons (stainless)
- Two staterooms & two heads with showers
- Hull Material: Fiberglass
- Displacement: 31,860 lbs.
- Full electronics
- Water maker, generator, & inverter

Portside Navigation Station

Starboardside Main Salon

Galley

DAN & MARSHA BREWER

My husband Dan and I were desert rats. We met, married, raised our children, and retired from what used to be a small town in the California high desert.

Our only experience with boats was a hot rod ski boat we owned in the 1970s. Then one summer we decided to take a vacation to the island of Antigua with some friends. We spent the first few days in a lovely condo on the island, but the next five days were spent on a beautiful 52-foot Benateau, with a captain, cruising around the island. My husband was in love! As soon as we got back home, he bought a 36-foot Columbia

Saber from the Boy Scouts. It was in horrible shape and I asked him if he was out of his mind. My husband is very handy and talented and it didn't take him long to turn a sow's ear into a silk purse. When he got finished, she was a beauty! With a 6-foot beam, she was very narrow and fast. She was also very forgiving on the ocean and so we quickly learned to sail. We kept her for two years, and then sold her.

It was time to move up to a bigger boat! Again, Dan found a fixer-upper and, again, I thought he was nuts. *Seaductress* was a 45-foot Excalibur, a considerably larger investment, and in a lot worse shape. I should have known better than to doubt him. He worked his magic once again and we ended up with an absolutely gorgeous yacht. We have many memories of cruising around the Channel Islands on her with some great trips to Catalina. The only trouble was that I wanted something a little larger, maybe with a bigger galley and, I thought, a second head would be nice. So we sold her.

We had been looking for the "perfect boat" for about a year and were getting discouraged. We knew we wanted a traditional-style yacht such as a Force 50 or a Formosa, but weren't having any luck. We'd made offers on a few, but it never worked out. Either the owners changed their minds or they wanted more than we were willing to pay. Then, one day, Dan spotted an ad in one of the "yachts for sale" magazines for a Formosa Puvioux 47 in San Francisco. So, the following weekend, we hopped in our '96 Corvette and took off for the Bay Area.

We got as far as the Tehachapi Mountains and blew the transmission in the car. Of course, it was just barely out of warranty. We had it towed into Bakersfield and left it at the Chevy dealership for repair. We rented a car and took off again. Finally, we reached the marina and walked down the dock to meet with the yacht broker. There, anchored in her slip, was *Nighthawk* and it was love at first sight. She was beautiful! Oh sure, she needed a lot of TLC, but even I could see what she would look like with a little love and elbow grease. She was a little out of our budget, but the owner and the broker worked with us and we bought her.

Nighthawk was originally built for, and owned by, the actor Sylvester Stallone in 1980-81. He had a lot of cool custom things done that make her unique. She has some lovely inlaid woodwork in the main salon and a beautiful, huge mirror with a hawk engraved in gold-leaf over the main settee. Stallone's favorite colors were gold and black and he used them throughout the yacht. The settees were all black leather and gold and black on the window curtains and bedspreads. However, it was a bit faded and worn.

Stallone originally sold the boat to a young man named Scott Smith who was the lead singer for the

Canadian rock group Loverboy. Later, he was lost at sea on another boat during a squall off the coast of San Francisco. There were two other owners for *Nighthawk* before we bought her and they all tried to keep the "flavor" of the boat as when Stallone had owned her. We have also tried to retain that look, however, we've lightened the interior by replacing the black leather with cream leather, replaced the curtains with cream-colored silk, and upgraded the heads and the galley. We've turned her into a very comfortable live-aboard yacht.

After we retired, we sold our house and moved aboard *Nighthawk*, living in Ventura, California for six years. Then we went cruising down to Baja, California and up the Sea of Cortez to San Carlos, Mexico. We lived on her in San Carlos for a year and a half until my mother became too ill with Alzheimer's to live alone.

At this point, we sold my mother's house in California and moved her with us to Temple, Texas, where we took care of her until her death in January 2015.

In my opinion, there is nothing better than the boating lifestyle. My only regret is that we didn't live aboard earlier and raise and home school our children on the boat. Also, Dan and I have found the boating community to be a close-knit group of people who go out of their way to help each other. Everywhere we've anchored or been in a slip, we've made friendships that have lasted for years.

Cruising from San Francisco down the California coast and the Mexican Baja, around Cabo San Lucas and up into the Sea of Cortez, we've seen amazing sea life; hundreds of giant multicolored jellyfish undulating just under the surface of the water as far as the eye can see; group after group of flying fish that land in our dingy and on our boat; graceful herds of manta rays that jump through the air like prehistoric birds; enormous sperm whales, hump-backed whales, and killer whales. Every time the dolphins swim with the boat, it never gets old. It's always as exciting as the first time.

It was our dream to continue cruising down the coast of Central America and eventually take our boat through the Panama Canal and do some cruising in the Gulf of Mexico and the Atlantic Ocean. However, due to some health issues, our plan now is to have *Nighthawk* shipped overland from San Carlos to Corpus Christi, Texas, and move aboard her again. There, I am sure we'll find new adventures while living aboard our beautiful yacht.

ANTHONY ALCOCK

THE HOWEYS

"We truly love living aboard our fishing seiner and, after the adventuresome life we live, there is no way we could handle traditional 9-5 jobs."

PACIFIC PREDATOR

58-foot Fishing Seiner

- Overall length 58', Beam 21'
- Aluminum hull
- Propulsion: 400HP diesel engine
- Other: Hydraulics for the various winches
- 20' Aluminum Net Boat with 400 HP diesel

Dining Room

Galley

BRYAN & DANA HOWEY

I have been in the fishing industry all my life. My wife, Dana, holds a degree in architecture and design and has several renowned homes to her credit.

Once we had decided to spend our lives together, we looked at how we could have the most time with each other, doing something that we both enjoyed. We chose commercial fishing.

I had grown up in Alaska and it provided seasonal employment and the opportunity to go travel in the off season, typically in three- to four-month chunks.

We use the working seasons like a savings account, giving us the time and money for the off season.

We are now on our sixth boat. All were 58 feet in length, which is the maximum allowed for salmon fishing. We also, at one time, had a seventy footer which we used for "Tendering." This is a process whereby you act as a service to other fishing vessels by transporting their fish back to port for processing and also supplying provisions and other services for their crew.

We actually got started in the year 2000, when Dana moved to Alaska from Florida. At that point, I became a skipper. Since then, we have been working up to a boat that can be effective at fishing anywhere from the Aleutian Islands to San Diego. It's difficult to get a boat that is comfortable and can do all of this. For example, a friend of ours just had one custom made, and it cost him $4.5 million. We paid $1 million for ours and, of course, we have put more into it since then.

A major cost is for permits. For example, the permit to fish salmon in Alaska is $250,000. The permit to fish squid in California is $1.4 million or more depending on the amount of tonnage on the permit. If you also wish to fish crab, it will cost you another $500,000 with permits and different fishing gear. To effectively string all the fishing opportunities together, you need all of these licenses. This way, you can cover all your options because when one type of fishing is in, another may be out.

We have a house in Sitka, Alaska, where we currently spend very little of our time. Dana designed and built it. It is gorgeous with teak wooden floors. We have spent only some three months in our house in the last two years. Our friends love us, as they get to use it and enjoy it, including our cars! In 2013, we did the salmon fishery out of Valdez, the sardine fishery out of Astoria, and then came down and hit the squid fishing here in Southern California.

When we started, it was tough because of the enormous expense involved. We began with a wooden boat with no autopilot and no lights. We went to Vancouver, where there were Russian shipwrights who specialized in wood boats. The boat needed quite a bit of work. We changed out some forty planks and a couple of ribs.

That first year, 2000, we fished for salmon in Alaska. This was Dana's first experience on a fishing boat. We worked with this boat for some four years. There was a lot of manual work because we did not have the latest winches and other gear.

Unfortunately, we lost this boat one evening in October 2004.

Unknown to us, when we were in Hawaii a few months earlier, our shore power cord had parted in a storm so that it wasn't making a full connection. This caused many of the metal boat fasteners to disintegrate which, in turn, caused several of the plank fasteners to fall apart. At the time, with only the two of us on board, we were heading up the Chatham Straits in Alaska when the bilge alarms started sounding. By the time I got down to see what was happening, we had some three feet of water in the boat. I ran up and ripped out the GPS and Dana was calling the Coast Guard. Luckily, we had a small inflatable dinghy. We were some four miles from shore and I turned the boat to head in that direction. The water in Chatham Strait is very deep—some 400 plus fathoms—so anchoring was not an option. I headed into a tiny cove. At this point, the engine was still running in spite of being totally underwater. I set the anchor in about 40 fathoms and, by this time, the Coast Guard was hovering above us. Dana climbed into the dinghy while I tried to do everything that I could think of to save our boat. I tried to convince the Coast Guard to throw us the pumps, but they ordered me off the vessel. Sure enough, just after I jumped in the dinghy, she sank with the "Crab Lights" still blazing underwater! Obviously, the generator, caught in an air pocket, was still running. It was only some 40 minutes from when the problem hit us that she sank. We had insurance but, because we hadn't reported a change of fisheries, they did not cover us. In hindsight, it was an amazing team effort. We really kept our cool and did everything we could to save her.

It took us a while to recover from this, financially and otherwise. We bought a 68-foot tender boat and did "tendering" for a while. This was actually a very pleasant time for us. My daughter, now graduated from college, was with us and we had a good time basically catering to a number of smaller fishing vessels. We did everything for them, allowing them to just fish. We were essentially their lifeline. We did their finances, cooking, provisioning, and even fixed their boats. It was actually a very enjoyable time in our life together, kind of idyllic in many ways.

We eventually invested in a fish company up in Alaska. We plan to open one here soon in Ventura. This has gone extremely well, as it is all fisherman-owned. It has enabled us to cut out the processors and do it ourselves.

Eventually, we plan to buy a large 60-foot plus catamaran to live on and hire a captain and crew to do what we do now. We could end up with more than one boat, but managing others brings its own challenges.

Our current boat can hold up to 82 tons of fish. With a full load, this can be quite lucrative. However, the ongoing cost of operation is high; the purchase of the boat and equipment ($2-4 million), expensive fishing licenses, ongoing maintenance (usually about 10% of the cost of the boat per year), plus crew and fuel.

As to our life aboard, we do get to spend our time together, usually assisted by a crew of three who have their own quarters. We try hard to select our crew so that we all get along with each other because, obviously, we are in pretty tight quarters.

Typically, we work hard for six months and then we have the time and money to go travel. Now that we are into squid, this may be more like 75% working. However, once we are off, we are free to go anywhere for a month or two at a time, which is great because we can really get to know the locals in other countries and spend time getting to understand their culture. For example, we were in Thailand for four months seven years ago and it was fabulous, probably our favorite trip.

One of our favorite "escapes" is to the hot springs in Baronoff, Alaska. They are adjacent to these massive waterfalls. You can sit in the warm water while watching these raging waters right next to you. At other times, we raft up to other fishing boats and we get a party going with wine, food, and live music. Dana is a real gourmet cook, so that, food-wise, we live very well. Of course, when we are working, it is more than a full-time job for all of us; up at 4 a.m. for salmon fishing, then all night until morning for squid fishing.

We truly love living aboard our fishing seiner and, after the adventuresome life we live, there is no way we could handle traditional 9-5 jobs.

A SUMMARY OF LIVING ABOARD

There is no question that living on a floating vessel of any kind is a unique experience. It is certainly not for everyone but, for those who choose it, "Life at the End of a Rope" can be very rewarding. Here, in summary, are a few things to consider:

- At its best, living aboard can be a magical experience. You are in an attractive marine environment, surrounded by friendly people who have also chosen this lifestyle. The gentle movement of your home and the pleasant ocean breezes provide a tranquil escape from today's rat race.

- Unless you are in the very large yacht group, life aboard is about living in a compact environment. This means no space for non-essentials, places for only what you need, and a strong emphasis on "ship-shape" and tidiness. If there is more than you—a spouse, children, and/or pets—plan on very close relationships and an intimacy not experienced living in a house on solid ground. Everyone must adjust and adapt to cohabiting in a relatively very small space.

- Unless you have deep pockets, and most people don't, you need to quickly learn how to "fix it yourself." When out at sea or cruising the world, you have no choice anyway. Even if your floating home never leaves the dock, you will need to be somewhat self-sufficient, as boats need lots of TLC and ongoing maintenance. Most people, who live aboard, actually accept these ongoing tasks as enjoyable therapy and part of the whole program.

- One of the main attractions, of course, is the ability to take your home, and all that you own, with you to other places. This may be as simple as a short offshore trip or a cruise around the world. Naturally, as you can see in the previous pages, this brings its own series of adventures and misadventures.

For all those people thinking about it, and the many already doing so, I wish you much happiness in your *"Life at the end of a Rope."*

BOAT TERMINOLOGY – SIMPLIFIED

Courtesy of "nautical know how" with some modification and additions

A

ABAFT - Toward the rear (stern) of the boat. Behind.

ABEAM - At right angles to the keel of the boat, but not on the boat.

ABOARD - On or within the boat.

ADRIFT - Loose, not on moorings or towline.

AFT - Toward the stern of the boat.

AGROUND - Touching or fast to the bottom.

ALEE - Away from the direction of the wind. Opposite of windward.

ALOFT - Above the deck of the boat.

AMIDSHIPS - In or toward the center of the boat.

ANCHORAGE - A place suitable for anchoring in relation to the wind, seas, and bottom.

ASTERN - In back of the boat, opposite of ahead.

ATHWARTSHIPS - At right angles to the centerline of the boat; rowboat seats are generally athwartships.

AWEIGH - The position of anchor as it is raised clear of the bottom.

B

BATTEN DOWN - Secure hatches and loose objects both within the hull and on deck.

BEAM - The greatest width of the boat.

BEARING - The direction of an object expressed either as a true bearing as shown on the chart, or as a bearing relative to the heading of the boat.

BIGHT - The part of the rope or line, between the end and the standing part, on which a knot is formed.

BILGE - The interior of the hull below the floor-boards.

BITTER END - The last part of a rope or chain. The inboard end of the anchor rode.

BOOT TOP - A painted line that indicates the designed waterline.

BOW - The forward part of a boat.

BOW LINE - A docking line leading from the bow. Also a knot used to form a temporary loop in the end of a line.

BRIDGE - The location from which a vessel is steered and its speed controlled. "Control Station" is really a more appropriate term for small craft.

BRIGHTWORK - Varnished woodwork and/or polished metal.

BULKHEAD - A vertical partition separating compartments.

BUOY - An anchored float used for marking a position on the water or a hazard or a shoal and for mooring.

BURDENED VESSEL - That vessel which, according to the applicable Navigation Rules, must give way to the privileged vessel. The term has been superseded by the term "give-way."

C

CABIN - A compartment for passengers or crew.

CAPSIZE - To turn over.

CAST OFF - To let go.

CATAMARAN - A twin-hulled boat, with hulls side by side.

CHINE - The intersection of the bottom and sides of a flat or v-bottomed boat.

CHOCK - A fitting through which anchor or mooring lines are led. Usually U-shaped to reduce chafe.

CLEAT - A fitting to which lines are made fast. The classic cleat to which lines are belayed is approximately anvil-shaped.

CLOVE HITCH - A knot for temporarily fastening a line to a spar or piling.

COCKPIT - An opening in the deck from which the boat is handled.

COURSE - The direction in which a boat is steered.

CUDDY - A small shelter cabin in a boat.

CURRENT - The horizontal movement of water.

D

DEAD AHEAD - Directly ahead.

DEAD ASTERN - Directly aft.

DECK - A permanent covering over a compartment, hull, or any part thereof.

DINGHY - A small open boat. A dinghy is often used as a tender for a larger craft.

DISPLACEMENT - The weight of water displaced by a floating vessel, thus, a boat's weight.

DISPLACEMENT HULL - A type of hull that plows through the water, displacing a weight of water equal to its own weight, even when more power is added.

DOCK - A protected water area in which vessels are moored. The term is often used to denote a pier or a wharf.

DOUBLE-ENDER - A boat with two pointy ends

DRAFT - The depth of water a boat draws.

E

EBB - A receding current.

F

FATHOM - Six feet.

FENDER - A cushion, placed between boats, or between a boat and a pier, to prevent damage.

FIGURE EIGHT KNOT - A knot in the form of a figure eight, placed in the end of a line to prevent the line from passing through a grommet or a block.

FLARE - The outward curve of a vessel's sides near the bow. Also a distress signal.

FLUKE - The palm of an anchor.

FOLLOWING SEA - An overtaking sea that comes from astern.

FORE- Front of the boat

FOREPEAK - A compartment in the bow of a small boat.

FORWARD - Toward the bow of the boat.

FREEBOARD - The minimum vertical distance from the surface of the water to the gunwale.

G

GALLEY - The kitchen area of a boat.

GANGWAY - The area of a ship's side where people board and disembark.

GEAR - A general term for ropes, blocks, tackle, and other equipment.

GIVE-WAY VESSEL - A term used to describe the vessel which must yield in meeting, crossing, or overtaking situations.

GROUND TACKLE - A collective term for the anchor and its associated gear.

GUNWALE - The upper edge of a boat's sides.

H

HALYARD (HAILIARD) - A line used to hoist a ladder sail or flag.

HARD CHINE - An abrupt intersection between the hull side and the hull bottom of a boat so constructed.

HATCH - An opening in a boat's deck fitted with a watertight cover.

HEAD - A marine toilet.

HEADING - The direction in which a vessel's bow points at any given time.

HEADWAY - The forward motion of a boat.

HELM - The wheel or tiller controlling the rudder.

HITCH - A knot used to secure a rope to another object or to another rope, or to form a loop or a noose in a rope.

HOLD - A compartment below deck in a large vessel, used solely for carrying cargo.

HULL - The main body of a vessel.

I

INBOARD - More toward the center of a vessel; inside; a motor fitted inside a boat.

INTRACOASTAL WATERWAY - ICW: bays, rivers, and canals along the coasts (such as the Atlantic and Gulf of Mexico coasts), connected so that vessels may travel without going into the sea.

J

JACOBS LADDER - A rope ladder, lowered from the deck, as when pilots or passengers come aboard.

JETTY - A structure, usually masonry, projecting out from the shore; a jetty may protect a harbor entrance.

K

KEEL - The centerline of a boat running fore and aft; the backbone of a vessel.

KNOT - A measure of speed equal to one nautical mile (6076 feet) per hour; a fastening made by interweaving rope to form a stopper, to enclose or bind an object, to form a loop or a noose, to tie a small rope to an object, or to tie the ends of two small ropes together.

L

LATITUDE - The distance north or south of the equator measured and expressed in degrees.

LAZARETTE - A storage space in a boat's stern area.

LEE - The side sheltered from the wind.

LEEWARD - The direction away from the wind. (Opposite of windward.)

LEEWAY - The sideways movement of the boat caused by either wind or current.

LINE - Rope and cordage used aboard a vessel.

LOG - A record of courses or operation. Also, a device to measure speed.

LONGITUDE - The distance in degrees east or west of the meridian at Greenwich, England.

LUBBER'S LINE - A mark or permanent line on a compass indicating the direction forward parallel to the keel when properly installed.

M

MARLINSPIKE - A tool for opening the strands of a rope while splicing.

MIDSHIP - Approximately in the location equally distant from the bow and stern.

MOORING - An arrangement for securing a boat to a mooring buoy or a pier.

N

NAUTICAL MILE - One minute of latitude; approximately 6076 feet - about 1/8 longer than the statute mile of 5280 feet.

NAVIGATION - The art and science of conducting a boat safely from one point to another.

O

OUTBOARD - Toward or beyond the boat's sides. Or a detachable engine mounted on a boat's stern.

OVERBOARD - Over the side or out of the boat.

P

PIER - A loading platform extending at an angle from the shore.

PILE - A wood, metal, or concrete pole driven into the bottom. Craft may be made fast to a pile; it may be used to support a pier (see PILING) or a float.

PILING - Support, protection for wharves, piers etc.; constructed of piles (see PILE).

PILOTING - Navigation by use of visible references, the depth of the water, etc.

PLANING - A boat is said to be "planning" when it is essentially moving over the top of the water rather than through the water.

PLANING HULL - A type of hull shaped to glide easily across the water at high speed.

PORT - The left side of a boat looking forward.

PRIVILEGED VESSEL - A vessel which, according to the applicable Navigation Rule, has right-of-way (this term has been superseded by the term "stand-on").

Q

QUARTER - The sides of a boat aft of amidships.

QUARTERING SEA - Sea coming on a boat's quarter.

R

RODE - The anchor line and/or chain.

ROPE - In general, cordage as it is purchased at the store. When it comes aboard a vessel and is put to use it becomes line.

RUDDER - A vertical plate or board for steering a boat.

RUN - To allow a line to feed freely.

RUNNING LIGHTS - Lights required to be shown on boats underway between sundown and sunup.

S

SATELLITE NAVIGATION - A form of position finding using radio transmissions from satellites with sophisticated onboard automatic equipment.

SCOPE - Technically, the ratio of length of anchor rode in use to the vertical distance from the bow of the vessel to the bottom of the water. This is usually six to seven to one for calm weather and more scope in storm conditions.

SCREW - Boat's propeller.

SCUPPERS - Drain holes on deck, in the toe rail, or in bulwarks or (with drain pipes) in the deck itself.

SEA COCK - A through hull valve, a shut off on a plumbing or drain pipe between the vessel's interior and the sea.

SEAWORTHY - A boat or a boat's gear able to meet the usual sea conditions.

SECURE - To make fast.

SET - Direction toward which the current is flowing.

SOLE - Cabin or saloon floor.

SOUNDING - A measurement of the depth of water.

SPRING LINE - A pivot line used in docking, un-docking, or to prevent the boat from moving forward or astern while made fast to a dock.

SQUALL - A sudden, violent wind often accompanied by rain.

SQUARE KNOT - A knot used to join two lines of similar size. (Also called a reef knot.)

STAND-ON VESSEL - That vessel which has right-of-way during a meeting, crossing, or overtaking situation.

STARBOARD - The right side of a boat when looking forward.

STEM - The forward most part of the bow.

STERN - The after part of the boat.

STOW - To put an item in its proper place.

SWAMP - To fill with water, but not settle to the bottom.

T

THWARTSHIPS - At right angles to the centerline of the boat.

TIDE - The periodic rise and fall of water level in the oceans.

TILLER - A bar or handle for turning a boat's rudder or an outboard motor.

TOPSIDES - The sides of a vessel between the waterline and the deck; sometimes referring to onto or above the deck.

TRANSOM - The stern cross-section of a square stern boat.

TRIM - Fore and aft balance of a boat.

U

UNDERWAY - Vessel in motion, i.e., when not moored, at anchor, or aground.

V

V BOTTOM - A hull with the bottom section in the shape of a "V."

W

WAKE - Moving waves, track, or path that a boat leaves behind it, when moving across the waters.

WATERLINE - A line painted on a hull which shows the point to which a boat sinks when it is properly trimmed (see BOOT TOP).

WAY - Movement of a vessel through the water such as headway, sternway, or leeway.

WINDWARD - Toward the direction from which the wind is coming.

Y

YACHT - A pleasure vessel, a pleasure boat; in American usage the idea of size and luxury is conveyed, either sail or power.

YAW - To swing or steer off course, as when running with a quartering sea.

"Twenty years from now you will be more disappointed by the things that you didn't do than by the ones you did do. So throw off the bowlines. Sail away from the safe harbor. Catch the trade winds in your sails. Explore. Dream. Discover."

Mark Twain

CPSIA information can be obtained
at www.ICGtesting.com
Printed in the USA
FSOW03n1943180516
20617FS

9 780997 162202